The
TAURUS
Path

YOUR DAILY 2026 HOROSCOPE GUIDE

AMANDA M CLARKE

Copyright © Amanda M Clarke 2026
KORU Publishing

All rights reserved. All content, materials, and intellectual property in this book or any other platform owned by Koru Publishing are protected by copyright laws. This includes text, images, graphics, videos, audio, software, and any other form of content that may be produced by Koru Publishing.

No part of this content may be reproduced, distributed, or transmitted in any form or by any means without the prior written permission of Koru Publishing. This means that you cannot copy, reproduce, or use any of the content in this book for commercial or personal purposes without the express written consent of Koru Publishing.

Unauthorized use of any copyrighted material owned by Koru Publishing may result in legal action being taken against you. Koru Publishing reserves the right to pursue all available legal remedies against any individual or entity found to be infringing on its copyright.

In summary, Koru Publishing © 2024 holds exclusive rights to all the content produced by it, and any unauthorized use of such content will result in legal action.

KORU Publishing

KORU (Maori:NZ)
A symbol of spiritual growth and spiritual connection.

Rocky Point Townhouse, CHRISTMAS ISLAND, Western Australia 6798

ISBN: 978-1-923614-03-1

More on the Bookshelves at
www.theliteraryoracle.com

Disclaimer: The Taurus Path: Your daily 2026 horoscope guide book provides information on astrological readings and intuative interpretations, it is not intended as a substitute for professional advice, diagnosis, or treatment. The information contained in this book is provided for educational and entertainment purposes only and is not meant to be taken as specific advice for individual circumstances. The author and publisher make no representations or warranties with respect to the accuracy or completeness of the contents of this book and specifically disclaim any implied warranties of merchantability or fitness for a particular purpose. The reader should always consult with a licensed professional for any specific concerns or questions. The author and publisher shall not be liable for any loss or damage caused or alleged to have been caused, directly or indirectly, by the information contained in this book. The use of this book is at the reader's sole risk

More from Amanda Clarke
The Literary Oracle
www.theliteracyoracle.com

The "Daily Guidance" series offers an innovative approach to finding spiritual wisdom and practical advice. Each book in the series is a unique tool designed for daily introspection and decision-making. Readers are invited to meditate on a question or seek general guidance for the day, then flip to a random page in the book. The page they land on provides a personalized message from various spiritual sources, such as angels, tarot, or spirit animals. With each turn of the page, these books deliver insightful, positive messages and mantras to inspire personal growth and provide clarity on life's daily challenges and decisions.

Other books in this series:-
The Angelic Oracles
Daily Angel Tarot Reading
Mystic Tarot Cat
Oracle of the Tarot Cat
Vibes Unveiled
Spirit Animal Oracle
Answers from the Oracles
Messages from the Angels

Supporting Indie Authors

Love your daily guidance? You can grab more of my books direct from The Literary Oracle: www.theliteraryoracle.com

Buying direct means:
- Much better prices for you + free shipping.
- More support for me as an indie author
- More magical books in your hands

My books are also available worldwide through online bookstores, but direct purchases help keep the magic flowing.

Thank you for supporting indie creativity!

Scan me

Welcome to The Taurus Path: Your Daily 2026 Horoscope Guide — your grounded, steady, and heart-centred companion for the year ahead. Crafted for the patient, loyal, and quietly determined Taurus, this guide honours the way you move through life — with calm persistence, practical wisdom, and a love of both stability and beauty.

Inside, you'll find daily horoscopes paired with affirmations designed to align with your natural strengths. Each reading is here to support you as you navigate 2026 — whether you're building long-term security, deepening meaningful relationships, tending to your well-being, or creating a life filled with comfort, joy, and purpose.

This isn't about chasing trends or rushing ahead — it's about embracing your pace, trusting your instincts, and finding abundance in the simple, steady steps you take. As you turn each page, you'll receive clarity, encouragement, and gentle reminders from the stars, guiding you to trust both yourself and the path unfolding before you. Let this be the year you root deeply, grow steadily, and flourish in harmony with your heart and the cosmos.

The Answers You Seek,

Are Within

January 2026

Taurus
01-January-2026

Taurus, the year begins with a gentle but steady cosmic push urging you to release outdated expectations and embrace a refreshed mindset. Venus, your ruler, is stirring connections in both love and finance, making today an ideal moment to align your values with your long-term goals. Don't let the small distractions of others' dramas throw you off balance. Instead, ground yourself in practical steps—tidy a space, make a list, or plan your week. This isn't about rushing forward but about setting a steady pace that feels true to you.

Affirmation & Gratitude

I welcome this new year with steady grace, trusting my values and planting seeds of lasting abundance.

Taurus
02-January-2026

Today brings you a deeper sense of clarity, Taurus, especially around relationships. You may notice which bonds are uplifting and which drain your energy. The Moon highlights communication, encouraging you to speak truthfully, but also listen with patience. It's not about winning debates—it's about creating balance. A small conversation may lead to surprising understanding if you remain calm and open. Don't dismiss intuitive nudges; your inner voice is whispering the right path forward. Ground yourself in routine, but leave room for meaningful interactions that nurture your soul.

Affirmation & Gratitude

I honour the connections that bring peace and release those that no longer align with my heart's truth.

Taurus
03-January-2026

Taurus, today the stars spotlight your finances and personal worth. A sudden opportunity to improve your income may appear, but it requires you to step outside your usual comfort zone. Don't let fear of change keep you from progress. Remember, security isn't just about money—it's about self-trust and knowing your skills have value. Spend time reflecting on how you can make your talents more visible. The key is believing in your own power. The universe is aligning to reward steady, practical action taken now.

Affirmation & Gratitude

I believe in my skills, trusting that my work and talents attract prosperity and recognition.

Taurus
04-January-2026

You may feel torn between rest and productivity today, Taurus. The Moon encourages downtime, but Mars is pulling you toward action. Balance is your gift—find a rhythm that allows both. Perhaps tackle one key task, then give yourself permission to relax without guilt. Don't underestimate the power of quiet reflection; insights often come when you're still. A new perspective may arrive through a dream, meditation, or even a peaceful walk. Allow yourself to enjoy the softer pace of the day without feeling you must prove yourself.

Affirmation & Gratitude

I balance rest and action, trusting that both serve my highest growth and bring me strength.

Taurus
05-January-2026

Taurus, today is perfect for clearing away clutter—both physical and emotional. You've been holding onto more than you need, and the stars urge you to let go. What feels heavy or outdated no longer belongs in your space. A release today will invite fresh opportunities tomorrow. Relationships may also benefit from honest conversations about boundaries and needs. Don't be afraid to express your feelings; you'll be surprised at how freeing it is. Transformation doesn't always come in loud ways—sometimes it's the quiet act of letting go.

Affirmation & Gratitude

I release what no longer serves me and invite fresh energy, clarity, and freedom into my life.

Taurus
06-January-2026

The energy shifts today, Taurus, pushing you toward expansion. This may show up as learning, travel planning, or simply seeing life from a wider lens. Your practical nature prefers stability, but sometimes adventure calls. Say yes to something new—even if it's small, like reading a book outside your usual interests or trying a different route. The universe is inviting you to broaden your perspective. Growth doesn't require abandoning security; it means blending curiosity with grounded action. The stars are nudging you to trust the unknown with steady faith.

Affirmation & Gratitude

I embrace new experiences, knowing they expand my heart, mind, and spirit while keeping me grounded.

Taurus
07-January-2026

Taurus, today highlights partnerships. Whether in romance, friendship, or business, you're asked to look at how balance plays out. Are you giving more than you're receiving, or holding back when you should be more open? The stars encourage collaboration, but also healthy boundaries. A moment of honesty could strengthen trust, even if it feels uncomfortable at first. Don't be afraid to show vulnerability—it doesn't weaken you, it deepens your connections. Remember, harmony in relationships comes from authenticity, not perfection.

Affirmation & Gratitude

I allow honest connections to thrive, creating relationships built on mutual respect, balance, and truth.

Taurus
08-January-2026

Taurus, today your focus shifts to health, daily routines, and the way you take care of your body and mind. The cosmos encourages small but steady adjustments that will support you long-term. Perhaps it's preparing nourishing meals, moving your body with intention, or simply reorganising your schedule to ease unnecessary stress. Don't underestimate the ripple effect of minor changes—what feels like a small step today can become a strong foundation for your future. Pay attention to what your body tells you; it's speaking clearly now. Honour it, and you'll notice renewed strength.

Affirmation & Gratitude

I nurture myself with care and honour my body's wisdom, knowing each small step builds lasting well-being.

Taurus
09-January-2026

Your creative spark is ignited today, Taurus, as planetary alignments stir your imagination and encourage self-expression. This isn't about perfection or impressing others—it's about playing with ideas, colour, words, or music simply for the joy of it. You may feel drawn to hobbies, art, or even spontaneous adventures that remind you of your inner child. Romance is also favoured, with a playful tone infusing conversations and connections. If you've felt weighed down lately, today offers a chance to lighten your heart and rediscover joy in simple pleasures. Creativity is your healing medicine now.

Affirmation & Gratitude

I embrace creativity and joy, allowing playfulness and passion to guide my heart toward freedom and delight.

Taurus
10-January-2026

Taurus, your attention turns toward work and responsibility today. While you're not afraid of hard effort, the stars caution you to avoid pushing yourself beyond your natural rhythm. Instead, focus on smart organisation and prioritising what really matters. If you've been chasing too many tasks at once, streamline. Conversations with authority figures may surface—be clear, calm, and grounded in your values. Recognition is possible now, but it will come through consistent effort rather than flashy gestures. Remember, your strength is persistence and reliability. Trust that showing up steadily will open doors for you.

Affirmation & Gratitude

I move steadily forward, trusting persistence and organisation to bring me the success and recognition I deserve.

Taurus
11-January-2026

Today the Moon shines on your friendships, networks, and community ties. Taurus, you may feel called to connect with like-minded people or revisit goals you've set with others. Collaboration is highlighted, but so is the importance of knowing who truly has your back. Not every connection is meant to last forever, and you may sense shifts in your social circle. Follow your instincts—gravitate toward those who inspire, uplift, and encourage growth. Whether it's sharing a dream or lending support, your presence is valuable. The right people see your worth without you needing to prove it.

Affirmation & Gratitude

I attract supportive connections that celebrate who I am and encourage my growth and dreams.

Taurus
12-January-2026

A deeply introspective energy surrounds you today, Taurus. You may feel quieter, more contemplative, and drawn to your inner world. Use this time to reflect on recent choices and how they've shaped your current path. The cosmos is encouraging release—old fears, grudges, or doubts can be acknowledged and gently put to rest. Dreams may hold special messages; pay attention to what stirs beneath the surface. Though you may feel less social, this is a healing pause, not a setback. By allowing yourself this depth, you create space for renewal and clarity moving forward.

Affirmation & Gratitude

I honour stillness and reflection, trusting that my inner wisdom guides me toward peace and renewal.

Taurus
13-January-2026

Taurus, today you step into renewed confidence and self-assurance as the stars light up your first house of identity. You may feel a boost of energy that encourages you to take bold steps forward, whether in your appearance, personal goals, or simply the way you carry yourself. The world notices your steady presence, and opportunities may come your way because you've allowed yourself to be visible. This is a reminder that you don't need to force change—authenticity itself shines brightly. Trust your worth and let your grounded nature be your greatest strength.

Affirmation & Gratitude

I shine with authenticity, allowing my true self to be seen, valued, and celebrated.

Taurus
14-January-2026

Today highlights your resources, Taurus, both financial and personal. You may find yourself reviewing budgets, expenses, or ways to strengthen security. But the stars also remind you that true abundance isn't measured only in money—it's also your skills, talents, and connections. A conversation around shared resources or investments could arise; approach it with practicality and calm. You're building something stable for the future, and patience will reward you. Resist the urge to compare your path to others—you're on your own timeline. Steadiness is your gift, and today it pays off.

Affirmation & Gratitude

I value my resources and trust in my ability to create lasting security and abundance.

Taurus
15-January-2026

Taurus, today brings focus to communication, learning, and the way you share your thoughts with others. A conversation may spark a new idea, or you could find yourself drawn to writing, studying, or simply soaking up knowledge. Your natural practicality allows you to turn inspiration into something tangible, so don't dismiss even the smallest insight. Be mindful of your words, though—once spoken, they carry weight. Choose clarity and kindness over impatience. If you've been considering a short trip, planning now will benefit you later. The universe is opening channels for mental expansion.

Affirmation & Gratitude

I communicate with clarity, absorbing wisdom and sharing my words with honesty, kindness, and purpose.

Taurus
16-January-2026

The stars shine a light on your home and family life today, Taurus. Domestic matters may need your attention, whether that means household tasks, family conversations, or simply carving out time to rest in your sacred space. If emotions run high, stay grounded and approach matters with calm patience—your steadiness helps restore balance. A memory from the past may resurface, offering insight into how far you've come. Whether you're reorganising a room, cooking for loved ones, or sitting quietly, nurture the space that nurtures you. Stability at home becomes your anchor for growth outside.

Affirmation & Gratitude

I create peace and stability within my home, honouring it as the foundation for my strength and happiness.

Taurus
17-January-2026

Taurus, romance and creativity sparkle today. Whether partnered or single, your heart is ready to feel more joy, warmth, and expression. If you've been holding back, let your playful side emerge—sing, dance, paint, or simply laugh without restraint. A relationship could deepen through shared joy or lighthearted connection. This is not a day for heavy responsibility; instead, it invites fun, affection, and self-expression. Trust that when you follow your heart, others are drawn to your authentic glow. Your creativity is not frivolous—it's essential to keeping your spirit alive and thriving.

Affirmation & Gratitude

I embrace joy, love, and creativity, allowing my playful spirit to shine and uplift those around me.

Taurus
18-January-2026

Today asks you to focus on your health and daily balance. Taurus, it's time to tune into your body's rhythm and see where adjustments are needed. Are you resting enough? Drinking water? Honouring your body with movement? Even small shifts—stretching, walking, or eating mindfully—make a difference now. Work tasks may demand attention too, but don't let stress build unchecked. Creating a routine that blends productivity and well-being is your path forward. Remember, your body is the vessel through which all your dreams flow, and nurturing it is an investment in your future.

Affirmation & Gratitude

I respect my body's needs and create balance in my daily life, honouring health as my true wealth.

Taurus
19-January-2026

Taurus, the cosmos highlights relationships again, asking you to look at balance and reciprocity. A partner, friend, or colleague may seek your support, but check in with yourself first—are you giving too much? Or are you holding back from being fully open? The truth lies in honest connection, not overextending or withholding. Today encourages you to see partnerships as mirrors; what you notice in others may reflect something within you. By approaching conversations with kindness and courage, you strengthen trust. Relationships that are aligned will grow stronger under today's energy.

Affirmation & Gratitude

I welcome balanced, loving connections that reflect my truth and honour mutual respect and care.

Taurus
20-January-2026

Today may stir deeper emotions, Taurus, as the Moon highlights themes of intimacy, vulnerability, and shared resources. You may be asked to trust someone with your heart, money, or secrets, and though it feels exposing, leaning into trust can bring growth. If fears arise, face them gently—acknowledge, then release. Transformation is the gift here, but it requires letting go of control and embracing depth. This is also a good day for reviewing finances or agreements with honesty. Healing comes when you allow yourself to be seen fully, without hiding.

Affirmation & Gratitude

I trust the process of transformation and allow vulnerability to deepen love, healing, and understanding.

Taurus
21-January-2026

Taurus, a wave of optimism lifts you today as the stars encourage expansion, learning, and seeing life from a bigger perspective. This could mean planning future travels, signing up for a course, or simply opening your mind to fresh philosophies. Opportunities come when you're willing to step outside of the comfortable and consider what else is possible. Your earthy nature prefers security, but growth often means taking measured risks. Say yes to something inspiring today—it could shape the direction of your year. Your soul is asking for adventure.

Affirmation & Gratitude

I embrace new horizons with courage, trusting each experience expands my wisdom and joy.

Taurus
22-January-2026

Taurus, today's cosmic energy shines on your ambitions and long-term goals. You may feel inspired to take bold steps toward career advancement or finally map out the path you want for the year ahead. Recognition is possible if you've been consistent, but don't expect overnight results. Your earthy patience is your superpower, and others admire the stability you bring. Conversations with mentors or authority figures may surface—approach them with confidence and clarity. Trust that your reliability and dedication are being noticed. The seeds you plant today have the potential to flourish into lasting success.

Affirmation & Gratitude

I take steady steps toward my ambitions, knowing patience and persistence bring lasting success and recognition.

Taurus
23-January-2026

Today invites you to connect with friends, groups, or networks, Taurus. Collaborative energy is strong, and you may feel inspired by conversations with like-minded souls. Whether it's brainstorming with colleagues, reconnecting with old friends, or sharing ideas with your community, the exchange of energy lifts your spirit. Stay open to invitations, even if they're outside your comfort zone—you may meet someone who sparks inspiration or offers unexpected support. This is also a good day to set intentions for your role in a team. You don't have to do everything alone; unity strengthens you.

Affirmation & Gratitude

I welcome connections that inspire growth, collaboration, and joy, knowing I thrive when I share my journey with others.

Taurus
24-January-2026

Taurus, the stars guide you inward today. You may feel quieter, more reflective, and drawn to moments of solitude. Rather than resisting, embrace this as a chance to reset your spirit. Your dreams or intuition may bring guidance, so pay attention to symbols, nudges, or synchronicities. This is a day for rest, gentle self-care, and releasing worries you've carried too long. By allowing yourself to pause, you prepare for the fresh energy that's coming. Trust that not every day requires action—sometimes the most powerful progress is made in stillness and silence.

Affirmation & Gratitude

I honour rest and reflection, trusting that stillness restores my clarity and strengthens my spirit.

Taurus
25-January-2026

Energy lifts today, Taurus, as the Moon moves into your sign, spotlighting your confidence, appearance, and personal goals. You may feel a burst of vitality and a renewed sense of direction. This is the perfect time to start something new or make your presence known. Others notice your steady strength and grounded nature, and opportunities may appear simply because you're showing up authentically. If doubts creep in, remember that you don't need to rush; your steady pace is enough. Today is about embodying your worth and embracing the power of being yourself fully.

Affirmation & Gratitude

I shine with confidence, embracing my true self and stepping forward with strength and authenticity.

Taurus
26-January-2026

Taurus, today encourages a deeper look at your resources—both financial and emotional. You may feel motivated to organise budgets, review investments, or strengthen security. But the universe also reminds you that wealth isn't just money—it's the skills, resilience, and connections you carry. Someone may offer advice or propose a financial discussion, so be ready to approach with calm practicality. Don't let comparison undermine your confidence; your journey is unique. By honouring your values, you'll attract prosperity that feels aligned and lasting. Today is about trusting your ability to create abundance in your way.

Affirmation & Gratitude

I value my unique path and trust my ability to create lasting prosperity rooted in my true values.

Taurus
27-January-2026

Communication is highlighted today, Taurus. The stars encourage you to share your ideas openly, whether through a conversation, writing, or teaching. Your words carry weight and can bring clarity to others, but remember to listen as much as you speak. Someone may reveal information that helps you see things differently. Short trips or changes to your daily routine could bring new perspectives. Stay curious and open, even if it means stepping beyond your usual comfort zone. Inspiration flows when you embrace fresh viewpoints and trust the exchange of ideas.

Affirmation & Gratitude

I communicate with openness and curiosity, trusting my words and listening bring insight and connection.

Taurus
28-January-2026

Home and family matters come into focus today, Taurus. You may feel called to nurture your space or spend time reconnecting with loved ones. Domestic projects, from cooking a meal to rearranging furniture, can bring surprising comfort and grounding. If tensions arise in family conversations, use your calm patience to guide the atmosphere back to balance. Your home is not just a structure—it's the foundation of your energy. By tending to it, you create a sanctuary that sustains you. Focus on building warmth and security in your personal world today.

Affirmation & Gratitude

I create harmony in my home, knowing it supports my peace, stability, and growth.

Taurus
29-January-2026

Taurus, today your creativity and joy are highlighted. You may feel drawn to hobbies, art, or simply having fun for fun's sake. Romance also glimmers under today's skies, with opportunities to express affection more openly. If life has felt heavy, today is your chance to lighten the load and reconnect with laughter. Don't underestimate the healing power of play; it balances the serious responsibilities you often carry. Give yourself permission to indulge in simple pleasures—a walk, a song, or a heartfelt chat. Your soul thrives when it is allowed to shine with joy.

Affirmation & Gratitude

I embrace joy and creativity, allowing playfulness and love to uplift and heal my spirit.

Taurus
30-January-2026

Taurus, the stars turn your attention toward health, habits, and work routines. Today is ideal for addressing practical matters you may have avoided—meal planning, organising tasks, or streamlining your schedule. The cosmos supports small, steady actions that reduce stress and build long-term stability. Avoid overloading your plate; instead, focus on one or two manageable steps. If you've been feeling scattered, grounding yourself through routine will restore calm. Remember, productivity isn't about being busy—it's about aligning your daily habits with what truly matters. A little structure goes a long way today.

Affirmation & Gratitude

I align my daily routines with balance and purpose, trusting that small steps create lasting strength.

Taurus
31-January-2026

Relationships come into the spotlight today, Taurus. You may find yourself reflecting on the give-and-take within your partnerships. The stars ask you to consider: are your connections balanced? If you've been overextending, it's time to step back and allow others to meet you halfway. If you've been holding back, the universe nudges you to open up more honestly. Harmony doesn't come from silence—it comes from courageous communication. Whether in love, friendship, or business, today supports creating bonds built on trust and respect. Vulnerability can strengthen ties when handled with care.

Affirmation & Gratitude

I create balance in my relationships, allowing honesty and respect to deepen trust and harmony.

February 2026

Taurus
01-February-2026

Taurus, today invites you to explore the depths of intimacy, shared resources, and personal transformation. The Moon highlights hidden emotions and may stir matters around finances or trust. You're encouraged to look beneath the surface, facing fears or insecurities that have lingered too long. Healing is possible now, but it requires honesty with yourself and others. Don't shy away from vulnerability; it opens the door to growth. Financially, reviewing agreements or commitments brings clarity. Trust that transformation often starts in quiet, uncomfortable moments before it blossoms into strength and renewal.

Affirmation & Gratitude

I welcome transformation, trusting vulnerability to deepen love and guide me toward healing and empowerment.

Taurus
02-February-2026

A sense of expansion fills the air today, Taurus. You may feel inspired to learn, explore, or broaden your worldview. Whether through books, study, travel planning, or deep conversations, opportunities to expand your perspective surround you. Your earthy nature prefers stability, but the stars encourage you to stretch beyond familiar patterns. Growth doesn't mean abandoning security—it means blending your steady pace with curiosity and openness. Say yes to experiences that spark wonder; they will enrich your journey. The bigger picture becomes clearer when you allow yourself to step back and see it fully.

Affirmation & Gratitude

I open my mind to new horizons, trusting curiosity and learning to enrich my journey.

Taurus
03-February-2026

Taurus, today your focus shifts toward career and public life. Recognition for your steady efforts may appear, or a conversation with an authority figure could shape your next steps. You may feel pressure to perform, but remember, success doesn't come from rushing—it comes from consistency, a quality you embody naturally. Trust that your grounded nature is your strength, even in high-pressure environments. If doubts surface, remind yourself how far you've already come. A professional opportunity or responsibility today could set the stage for longer-term success, provided you approach with patience and clarity.

Affirmation & Gratitude

I trust my steady effort brings recognition and success, knowing persistence builds lasting achievements.

Taurus
04-February-2026

Taurus, friendships and community take centre stage today. The cosmos highlights your networks and reminds you of the strength found in shared goals. You may feel uplifted by like-minded people or inspired to contribute to a cause bigger than yourself. Collaboration brings momentum and joy now. If you've felt isolated, reconnecting with your tribe will restore balance. Remember, not every connection is meant to stay, but the ones that align with your values will endure. Open yourself to new ideas through teamwork—you'll find inspiration in the company of others.

Affirmation & Gratitude

I value my community and welcome connections that align with my values and inspire collective growth.

Taurus
05-February-2026

Taurus, today's energy draws you inward, encouraging solitude and reflection. The cosmos is asking you to rest, recharge, and reconnect with your inner wisdom. You may feel less social than usual, preferring quiet activities like journaling, meditating, or simply sitting with your thoughts. Pay attention to your dreams or subtle synchronicities—they hold valuable guidance. This is also a good day for releasing old burdens you've carried for too long. By allowing yourself space to pause, you strengthen your emotional and spiritual foundation. Stillness isn't wasted time—it's a powerful reset that prepares you for forward momentum.

Affirmation & Gratitude

I honour my need for rest and reflection, trusting that quiet moments restore my strength and clarity.

Taurus
06-February-2026

Taurus, the Moon lights up your sign today, bringing a surge of energy, confidence, and visibility. This is your moment to step forward with authenticity and embrace new beginnings. If you've been waiting for a sign to start something fresh—a project, a conversation, or even a change in appearance—the stars are aligned to support you. Others notice your steady presence and may be drawn to your calm authority. Don't be afraid to let yourself shine. Your grounded energy makes you magnetic, and doors may open simply because you're showing up as yourself.

Affirmation & Gratitude

I radiate confidence and embrace new beginnings, trusting my authenticity attracts opportunities aligned with my path.

Taurus
07-February-2026

Today, your focus turns to personal resources, Taurus—finances, skills, and the security you're building for the future. You may feel motivated to review budgets, organise accounts, or plan investments. But this is also about recognising your inner resources: your talents, resilience, and determination. Don't undervalue what you bring to the table. A practical plan you begin today could pay off in steady, long-term results. Resist comparing yourself to others; your financial and personal journey is uniquely yours. Ground yourself in gratitude for what you already have as you take steps toward abundance.

Affirmation & Gratitude

I value my resources and trust my steady efforts create lasting financial and personal security.

Taurus
08-February-2026

Taurus, communication takes centre stage today. Conversations may hold greater weight than usual, so choose your words thoughtfully. You could find yourself writing, teaching, or sharing ideas that resonate strongly with others. Listen as much as you speak; valuable insights come through balanced exchanges. Short trips, errands, or learning opportunities may arise, opening your perspective. Be mindful not to get stuck in rigid thinking—the stars encourage flexibility in how you process and express information. Your grounded nature helps you communicate with clarity, but an open mind ensures your wisdom continues to grow.

Affirmation & Gratitude

I communicate with clarity and openness, trusting that my words and ideas create meaningful connections.

Taurus
09-February-2026

Home and family matters surface today, Taurus, and you may feel pulled to create more peace in your domestic world. Whether you're handling practical tasks like cleaning, repairs, or organising, or emotional matters within your family, the cosmos supports building harmony. A conversation with a loved one could bring understanding, provided you remain calm and patient. This is also a wonderful day to reconnect with your roots, honour traditions, or simply nurture your own space. When your home feels grounded and stable, it reflects in every area of your life.

Affirmation & Gratitude

I create harmony in my home and cherish the stability it provides for my growth.

Taurus
10-February-2026

Your creativity and playful side sparkle today, Taurus. The universe encourages you to express joy through hobbies, romance, or simply indulging in what lights up your heart. If you've been feeling stuck, creative expression offers release and inspiration. Don't dismiss fun as unproductive—laughter and play restore your spirit. Romance is favoured, whether deepening existing bonds or opening your heart to new possibilities. Your grounded energy combined with lightheartedness makes you magnetic now. Allow yourself to experience beauty, colour, and joy in whatever form they arrive today.

Affirmation & Gratitude

I embrace joy, creativity, and love, knowing they enrich my spirit and connect me to life's beauty.

Taurus
11-February-2026

Taurus, today focuses on your health, habits, and daily responsibilities. You may feel called to bring order to areas that have slipped out of balance. The stars support small, practical adjustments—organising your schedule, preparing healthy meals, or finding time for exercise. Don't push for perfection; consistency is what matters most. If work tasks demand attention, tackle them methodically rather than rushing. Balance is key today—blend productivity with self-care. By grounding yourself in routine, you create stability that supports your long-term goals and overall well-being.

Affirmation & Gratitude

I honour balance in my daily life, knowing consistency and care create strength and stability.

Taurus
12-February-2026

Taurus, relationships are highlighted today as the cosmos draws attention to how you give and receive within partnerships. You may feel prompted to look at whether your connections are balanced, fair, and nurturing. A partner or close friend might need more of your presence, but be careful not to overextend yourself. True harmony is found in honest communication, not self-sacrifice. If single, this energy may stir your desire for connection or highlight patterns in past relationships. Use today to strengthen bonds by being open, authentic, and willing to listen with your whole heart.

Affirmation & Gratitude

I honour balance in my relationships, allowing honesty and respect to guide my connections.

Taurus
13-February-2026

Taurus, today invites you to explore deeper emotional or financial matters. The Moon stirs themes of intimacy, trust, and transformation. Conversations around shared resources, money, or emotional needs may arise, and while they might feel intense, they can also be healing. You're asked to look beneath the surface, acknowledging fears or insecurities that may have held you back. By leaning into vulnerability, you open doors to profound connection and renewal. Financially, this is a good day to review joint commitments with care. Remember, transformation begins when you release what no longer supports your growth.

Affirmation & Gratitude

I trust transformation and allow vulnerability to bring healing, strength, and deeper connection.

Taurus
14-February-2026

Valentine's Day brings an expansive energy for you, Taurus, one that encourages growth, learning, and exploration. Whether partnered or single, this cosmic vibe pushes you to look at love and life through a bigger lens. Travel, study, or philosophical conversations could inspire your heart today. You may realise that love isn't confined to romance—it's also about adventure, laughter, and shared discovery. If you've been playing it safe, now is the time to say yes to something new. The universe is encouraging you to embrace the unknown and allow your heart to grow.

Affirmation & Gratitude

I welcome love and adventure in all forms, trusting growth comes from openness and curiosity.

Taurus
15-February-2026

Taurus, career and ambitions come to the forefront today. You may find yourself in the spotlight, with recognition possible for your steady efforts. Conversations with superiors or mentors could open doors to new opportunities, so approach them with confidence and clarity. While you prefer security over risk, the stars encourage you to stretch your professional boundaries. A step outside your comfort zone could lead to lasting growth. Trust your instincts but also lean into your patience—the rewards of your persistence are ripening. Today reminds you that your reliability is a powerful strength others value.

Affirmation & Gratitude

I step confidently into my ambitions, trusting my persistence and dedication lead to lasting success.

Taurus
16-February-2026

Your friendships and community ties are highlighted today, Taurus. The cosmos encourages you to lean into connections with like-minded souls who inspire you. A group project or collaborative effort could bring exciting progress, but be mindful of who truly supports your vision. Not every connection is meant to stay, and it's okay to gently release what no longer aligns. By surrounding yourself with uplifting people, you create momentum toward your goals. Social energy is high—say yes to invitations that feel expansive. The right tribe will energise you rather than drain you.

Affirmation & Gratitude

I attract supportive friendships and welcome connections that inspire growth and joy.

Taurus
17-February-2026

Taurus, today brings introspection and reflection. The Moon encourages you to retreat a little, recharge, and process emotions that may have surfaced recently. You may feel called to rest, journal, or meditate, allowing yourself space to listen to your intuition. This is also a powerful day for releasing worries or fears you've carried too long. Solitude can feel healing now, helping you reset before the energy shifts again. Trust that quiet time is productive in its own way—it strengthens your inner clarity. Sometimes stepping back is exactly what's needed for long-term progress.

Affirmation & Gratitude

I honour stillness and reflection, trusting that solitude restores clarity and strength.

Taurus
18-February-2026

The Sun moves into Pisces today, Taurus, spotlighting your friendships, goals, and dreams for the coming month. You may feel a renewed desire to connect with your community or revisit long-term aspirations. Conversations with friends could spark inspiration, and collaboration becomes a theme. Don't be afraid to share your vision—the universe supports your willingness to dream big now. While your earthy nature prefers what's practical, today asks you to blend vision with realism. The balance of dreaming and grounding creates true magic, helping you take meaningful steps toward your future.

Affirmation & Gratitude

I dream big while staying grounded, trusting my vision and steady steps to create lasting success.

Taurus
19-February-2026

Taurus, today relationships and partnerships may come into sharper focus as the Moon activates areas of commitment, balance, and reciprocity. Someone close to you could seek clarity or reassurance, and your natural steadiness can provide comfort. However, don't ignore your own needs in the process—harmony is built on fairness, not self-sacrifice. A conversation may help you both understand each other better, but it requires honesty and openness. If you're single, pay attention to interactions that spark curiosity; new connections may have long-term potential. This is a day for building stronger foundations in relationships.

Affirmation & Gratitude

I give and receive with balance, creating relationships that honour truth, fairness, and mutual respect.

Taurus
20-February-2026

Taurus, the energy today stirs deep emotions around intimacy, vulnerability, and trust. Financial or emotional entanglements may need your attention—be it joint finances, shared resources, or simply allowing yourself to lean on someone you trust. The stars encourage you to acknowledge fears instead of burying them. Transformation is possible when you're brave enough to let go of old wounds or outdated control. By embracing vulnerability, you strengthen bonds and open pathways for growth. Don't fear the process of change; it is shaping you into a more resilient and grounded version of yourself.

Affirmation & Gratitude

I embrace transformation, allowing vulnerability to guide me toward healing and deeper connection.

Taurus
21-February-2026

Optimism fills your day, Taurus, as the stars encourage you to think bigger, explore, and expand your perspective. This could mean diving into study, planning travel, or engaging in meaningful conversations that stretch your worldview. Your earthy nature loves stability, but growth requires fresh experiences. Today is a reminder that you can keep your roots strong while letting your branches stretch toward the sky. Say yes to opportunities that inspire learning or exploration. Each new perspective you gain adds richness to your journey. Trust that curiosity is a gift guiding your evolution.

Affirmation & Gratitude

I welcome new horizons with courage, trusting learning and exploration to enrich my life.

Taurus
22-February-2026

Taurus, career and public responsibilities come into the spotlight today. Recognition for your efforts may appear, or you may be called upon to take the lead in a situation. While this might feel like pressure, remember that your reliability and patience are exactly what people admire. Use today to showcase your skills, but don't rush or overcompensate—your steady approach already sets you apart. Long-term goals benefit from practical planning now. Trust that consistent action is far more effective than dramatic gestures. You're building a legacy through persistence and integrity, and today you see glimpses of that reward.

Affirmation & Gratitude

I step forward with confidence, trusting my steady effort builds a lasting legacy of success.

Taurus
23-February-2026

The Moon highlights friendships, groups, and community involvement today, Taurus. You may feel drawn to collaborate, share ideas, or reconnect with people who align with your dreams. Inspiration flows when you surround yourself with supportive energy. Be mindful of which connections energise you and which drain you—it's okay to step back from what no longer serves. A shared project or group intention may gain momentum now, reminding you that collective efforts often amplify results. Say yes to gatherings or discussions that feel expansive. You thrive when you know you're part of something bigger.

Affirmation & Gratitude

I welcome community and collaboration, trusting shared energy helps dreams grow stronger.

Taurus
24-February-2026

Taurus, today invites you into introspection and spiritual reflection. You may feel called to spend time alone, listening to your inner voice or reconnecting with your dreams. Intuition is heightened, so pay attention to subtle nudges and synchronicities. Use this quiet energy for meditation, journaling, or simply resting. Releasing emotional clutter clears the way for clarity and renewal. Though the day may feel low-energy on the surface, beneath it lies powerful healing potential. By honouring stillness, you restore your balance and strengthen your connection to your higher self.

Affirmation & Gratitude

I honour rest and reflection, trusting inner wisdom to guide me toward peace and renewal.

Taurus
25-February-2026

Energy shifts today as the Moon enters your sign, Taurus, giving you a fresh burst of vitality and self-confidence. You may feel more visible, ready to take action, or eager to express yourself authentically. Others notice your grounded presence, and opportunities may come simply because you're showing up as yourself. This is a perfect time to set personal intentions, update goals, or take bold first steps. Don't let self-doubt creep in—your earthy steadiness already makes you magnetic. Today is about trusting who you are and moving forward with courage.

Affirmation & Gratitude

I shine with authenticity and step confidently into opportunities aligned with my true self.

Taurus
26-February-2026

Taurus, today your focus turns to your personal resources—money, possessions, and self-worth. You may feel motivated to organise finances, review budgets, or consider how to strengthen long-term security. Yet this isn't only about material matters; it's also about recognising your skills and talents as valuable resources. Don't underestimate the unique gifts you bring to the table. Confidence in yourself attracts opportunities that reflect your worth. Be cautious of comparing yourself to others—it undermines your steady progress. Ground yourself in gratitude for what you already have, while opening to new ways of creating abundance.

Affirmation & Gratitude

I value my skills and trust that my steady efforts build lasting prosperity.

Taurus
27-February-2026

Taurus, communication takes centre stage today. Conversations may bring clarity, but only if you listen as much as you speak. You could find yourself writing, learning, or sharing ideas that carry influence with others. A message or unexpected news could shift your perspective. Be mindful of rigid thinking—the stars encourage flexibility and curiosity. This is also a favourable day for short trips or errands that inspire fresh insights. If you've been meaning to reach out to someone, now is the time. Words hold power today, so use yours with thoughtfulness and care.

Affirmation & Gratitude

I communicate with clarity and openness, trusting that meaningful dialogue deepens connection.

Taurus
28-February-2026

Home and family matters take priority today, Taurus. You may feel pulled to nurture your space or handle domestic responsibilities that bring order and comfort. Whether it's tending to practical repairs, cooking, or simply creating a peaceful atmosphere, your home becomes your sanctuary. Emotional conversations with family members could arise, offering opportunities for understanding if approached with patience. Honour your roots and traditions, but also allow room for creating new ones that reflect who you are becoming. When your home is in balance, you feel more grounded in every other aspect of your life.

Affirmation & Gratitude

I create harmony in my home, honouring it as the foundation of peace and security.

March 2026

Taurus
01-March-2026

Creativity and joy sparkle today, Taurus. You're encouraged to step into playfulness, whether through artistic hobbies, romance, or simply enjoying life's pleasures. If you've been carrying heavy responsibilities, today offers a chance to lighten your spirit. Express yourself freely—sing, dance, paint, or laugh without restraint. Romantic energy is strong, so open your heart to affection and connection. Remember, joy is not a distraction from life's duties; it's a vital part of your well-being. Allow yourself to experience beauty in its simplest forms, and you'll feel rejuvenated from the inside out.

Affirmation & Gratitude

I embrace joy and creativity, allowing play to restore my heart and spirit.

Taurus
02-March-2026

Taurus, today the cosmos reminds you of the importance of routines and self-care. You may feel called to organise your schedule, refine habits, or make practical adjustments that support your long-term health. Small steps—like preparing nourishing meals, moving your body, or setting clear boundaries with work—make a noticeable difference now. The key is consistency, not perfection. If you've been putting off a task, today is the time to tackle it steadily. By creating balance between responsibility and rest, you build resilience that carries you forward with strength.

Affirmation & Gratitude

I create balance in my daily routines, honouring consistency as the key to lasting wellness.

Taurus
03-March-2026

Relationships come under focus today, Taurus. The stars highlight your partnerships, asking you to look honestly at balance, trust, and commitment. A heart-to-heart may be needed, and while it may feel vulnerable, it strengthens understanding. If single, pay attention to new connections that may carry long-term significance. Remember, relationships are not about perfection but about mutual growth. Be mindful not to give more than you receive, or to hold back when your heart wants to open. Authenticity is the bridge to deeper, healthier connections now.

Affirmation & Gratitude

I create harmony in my relationships through honesty, balance, and openness.

Taurus
04-March-2026

Taurus, transformation and renewal are themes today. Matters around intimacy, shared resources, or deeper emotions may surface, asking for attention. Though it may feel intense, this is an opportunity for growth. The cosmos encourages you to release old fears and step into vulnerability, trusting that letting go makes space for healing. Financially, joint commitments may need review—be honest with yourself and others. Emotionally, this is a powerful day for recognising how far you've come. Transformation isn't always comfortable, but it is always necessary. Embrace it with your steady courage.

Affirmation & Gratitude

I embrace transformation, trusting release and renewal to guide me to strength and clarity.

Taurus
05-March-2026

Taurus, optimism lifts your spirit today as the stars encourage you to broaden your perspective. This may come through travel planning, study, or simply seeing the bigger picture in your current situation. You've been focused on details lately, but today invites you to stretch beyond routine and consider what's truly possible. Inspiration flows when you allow yourself to dream without immediately worrying about the "how." The universe is reminding you that expansion doesn't require abandoning stability—it's about blending vision with your steady nature. Say yes to growth opportunities, no matter how small.

Affirmation & Gratitude

I welcome growth and adventure, trusting that new experiences expand my wisdom and joy.

Taurus
06-March-2026

Taurus, career and public life are spotlighted today. Recognition for your persistence may arrive, or you may be called to take responsibility in a visible way. This could feel like added pressure, but your grounded energy makes you well-equipped to handle it. Today is about aligning your long-term goals with your daily actions. Don't rush; success comes from consistency and integrity. A conversation with a superior or mentor may open doors—approach it with clarity and calm confidence. You are building a legacy, one reliable step at a time.

Affirmation & Gratitude

I step forward with confidence, trusting my persistence and integrity to shape lasting success.

Taurus
07-March-2026

Friendships, teamwork, and community ties come into focus today, Taurus. You may feel inspired to connect with like-minded souls, share ideas, or work on collective goals. A group project may gain momentum, or you may find new opportunities through networking. Be discerning, though—not every connection needs to stay. Gravitate toward those who energise and inspire you rather than drain your energy. By aligning with supportive people, your dreams gain strength. Social energy is high, so don't shy away from gatherings that bring joy and inspiration.

Affirmation & Gratitude

I attract supportive connections that encourage growth, joy, and collaboration.

Taurus
08-March-2026

Taurus, today invites reflection and rest. You may feel drawn to quiet activities that allow your mind and spirit to reset—journaling, meditating, or simply spending time in solitude. Pay attention to dreams or subtle messages, as your intuition is heightened now. If emotions surface, let them move through you rather than suppressing them. Restoring balance within yourself allows you to face the coming days with greater clarity. This pause isn't wasted—it's essential for your growth and resilience. Trust that stillness today prepares you for progress tomorrow.

Affirmation & Gratitude

I honour rest and reflection, trusting that stillness restores my clarity and strength.

Taurus
09-March-2026

The Moon lights up your sign today, Taurus, boosting your energy, visibility, and confidence. You may feel ready to step into new beginnings or assert yourself more strongly. This is a perfect day to set personal intentions, take bold first steps, or make changes that reflect your true self. Others notice your calm authority, and opportunities may appear because you're showing up authentically. Doubts may try to creep in, but your grounded nature reminds you that steady progress is enough. Today is about claiming your place and moving forward with courage.

Affirmation & Gratitude

I shine with authenticity, stepping confidently into opportunities aligned with my truth.

Taurus
10-March-2026

Taurus, your focus shifts to resources today—both material and personal. You may review finances, organise budgets, or think about how to create greater stability. But remember, your skills, resilience, and determination are just as valuable as money. Don't downplay what you bring to the table. A practical step taken today could support long-term abundance. Avoid comparing your progress with others; your steady path is uniquely yours. By trusting your abilities and valuing your worth, you attract opportunities that reflect prosperity and security.

Affirmation & Gratitude

I value my worth and trust my steady efforts to create lasting abundance.

Taurus
11-March-2026

Communication is emphasised today, Taurus. Conversations could bring clarity, inspiration, or even healing if you're open to listening as much as you speak. Writing, teaching, or learning may also be highlighted—your words carry weight now, so use them wisely. Be mindful of rigid thinking; flexibility allows you to gain fresh insights. Short trips or unexpected errands could also open new opportunities. The universe is encouraging you to stay curious and engaged, because wisdom often comes through simple exchanges when you least expect it.

Affirmation & Gratitude

I communicate with clarity and curiosity, trusting that meaningful exchanges bring insight and connection.

Taurus
12-March-2026

Taurus, home and family matters take the spotlight today. You may feel a pull to nurture your living space, repair something practical, or strengthen bonds with loved ones. Emotions could run deeper than usual, especially around roots, memories, or traditions. This is a good day to bring balance to your home life—whether through cleaning, cooking, or simply spending quality time together. If challenges arise, your calm steadiness can restore harmony. Remember, when your home feels peaceful, it becomes the foundation that supports everything else you do.

Affirmation & Gratitude

I create peace and balance in my home, honouring it as the foundation of my strength.

Taurus
13-March-2026

Creativity and joy come alive today, Taurus. You may feel inspired to paint, write, dance, or indulge in any form of self-expression that lights up your soul. Romance is also favoured, whether through playful moments with a partner or opening your heart to love's possibilities. Don't underestimate the healing power of fun—it restores energy that routine and responsibility often drain. Allow yourself to laugh, explore beauty, and feel pleasure without guilt. Life isn't only about productivity; it's also about savouring joy.

Affirmation & Gratitude

I embrace creativity, joy, and love, knowing they enrich my spirit and bring balance to my life.

Taurus
14-March-2026

Taurus, your focus shifts toward health, routines, and daily responsibilities. You may feel motivated to tidy your schedule, refine habits, or take steps toward greater balance. This isn't about perfection—it's about building sustainable practices that keep you grounded. A small act of organisation today can ripple into greater clarity tomorrow. Be mindful not to overload yourself; your steady pace is your strength. Caring for your body through food, rest, and movement is especially favoured. Remember, consistency builds resilience, and today offers you the chance to set that tone.

Affirmation & Gratitude

I honour balance in my daily routines, trusting consistency to bring health and stability.

Taurus
15-March-2026

Partnerships come into focus today, Taurus. Whether in romance, friendship, or business, you're asked to consider the balance of give and take. A conversation may be needed to clarify expectations or strengthen trust. If single, this energy could highlight new opportunities to connect with someone meaningful. Harmony is possible, but it requires honesty, patience, and willingness to listen. Your grounded presence is a gift in relationships—it offers stability to others. Today, seek fairness and authenticity in your connections, and you'll find deeper understanding waiting for you.

Affirmation & Gratitude

I nurture balance and authenticity in my relationships, trusting honesty to deepen connections.

Taurus
16-March-2026

Deep transformation energy surrounds you today, Taurus. The cosmos highlights themes of intimacy, shared resources, and personal renewal. Emotions may run high, but they're guiding you toward clarity and release. Financial matters involving joint commitments may also surface—review them carefully. Spiritually, this is a powerful day for letting go of old fears, grudges, or patterns that no longer serve you. By facing what you've avoided, you create space for healing and growth. Transformation isn't always easy, but it brings lasting strength.

Affirmation & Gratitude

I embrace transformation and release what no longer serves, trusting renewal to bring strength.

Taurus
17-March-2026

Optimism flows today, Taurus, as the stars encourage learning, expansion, and seeing the bigger picture. You may feel inspired to explore new ideas, take a class, or plan travel that opens your horizons. Conversations with people from different backgrounds may spark exciting insights. Your earthy nature prefers stability, but today asks you to mix it with curiosity. Growth comes when you step outside your comfort zone. Allow yourself to say yes to experiences that expand your worldview—you'll feel enriched and inspired.

Affirmation & Gratitude

I welcome growth and new perspectives, trusting curiosity to guide my journey.

Taurus
18-March-2026

Taurus, career matters and long-term goals are highlighted today. You may feel recognition for your steady efforts, or you might be asked to step into a leadership role. While this could feel daunting, your patience and reliability are exactly what others admire. Use today to review your professional path and ensure it aligns with your values. Practical planning now sets the stage for success later. Remember, success isn't about rushing ahead—it's about building a legacy with integrity and persistence.

Affirmation & Gratitude

I step confidently toward my goals, trusting persistence and patience to shape lasting success.

Taurus
19-March-2026

Taurus, friendships and community ties are emphasised today. You may feel called to connect with groups or individuals who share your values and vision. Collaborative projects are favoured, and a conversation with a friend could bring fresh ideas or support. However, you may also notice where certain connections have run their course. Be discerning—focus on those that energise and uplift you. Your steady loyalty is a gift, but don't spend it on relationships that drain your spirit. The right tribe will strengthen your dreams and inspire your growth.

Affirmation & Gratitude

I attract supportive connections that uplift, inspire, and encourage my dreams.

Taurus
20-March-2026

Taurus, today invites you into reflection and stillness. The Moon highlights your inner world, and you may feel drawn to solitude, meditation, or journaling. Dreams or intuitive nudges may bring clarity, so listen closely to subtle signs. Emotions could rise to the surface, asking for release. Rather than pushing through, give yourself permission to pause. Stillness today is powerful—it helps you reset before stepping into fresh energy tomorrow. Trust that rest is not wasted time but a vital part of your growth.

Affirmation & Gratitude

I honour rest and reflection, trusting quiet moments to restore clarity and balance.

Taurus
21-March-2026

The Sun moves into Aries today, lighting up the most private part of your chart. Taurus, this marks a month of closure, release, and preparation before your birthday season begins. You may feel more introspective, sensing what needs to be let go before you step into new beginnings. Take stock of habits, patterns, or relationships that no longer serve you. Trust that letting go creates space for what's to come. This is a time for healing, reflection, and gentle preparation, not rushing ahead.

Affirmation & Gratitude

I release what no longer serves me, preparing my spirit for renewal and growth.

Taurus
22-March-2026

Taurus, today the Moon enters your sign, bringing fresh energy, confidence, and visibility. You may feel ready to take action on personal goals or simply show up more authentically. Others notice your calm strength, and opportunities may come your way because of it. This is an excellent day for setting intentions, beginning projects, or embracing a fresh perspective. If doubts arise, remind yourself of the steadiness that defines you. Today is about embodying your worth and trusting your presence has power.

Affirmation & Gratitude

I shine with confidence and step forward authentically, trusting my steady nature to guide me.

Taurus
23-March-2026

Taurus, your focus turns to personal resources today—money, possessions, and self-worth. You may feel prompted to review finances, create a plan, or explore ways to strengthen stability. But this is also about recognising your personal value. The talents and skills you often take for granted are sources of abundance. Don't underestimate yourself or fall into comparison with others—your path is unique. A practical step you take now could pay off in the long run. Confidence in yourself is key to unlocking opportunities.

Affirmation & Gratitude

I value my worth and trust my steady steps to create abundance.

Taurus
24-March-2026

Communication is highlighted today, Taurus. You may find yourself in important conversations, writing, or sharing ideas with others. Be mindful of your words—once spoken, they carry weight. Listen carefully as well, because someone may share wisdom that shifts your perspective. Short trips, errands, or unexpected exchanges could spark inspiration. Your grounded presence helps you communicate with calm and clarity, but stay flexible—new insights come when you allow yourself to see things differently. Curiosity is your ally today.

Affirmation & Gratitude

I communicate with clarity and openness, welcoming new ideas that inspire growth.

Taurus
25-March-2026

Taurus, home and family themes come into focus today. You may feel pulled to nurture your living space, handle domestic responsibilities, or connect more deeply with loved ones. This is a day to bring balance to your private world, making it a source of comfort and stability. Conversations with family members may arise—stay patient and grounded, as your steady presence helps ease tension. Even small acts like cooking, cleaning, or rearranging furniture can refresh your energy. Remember, a peaceful home creates the foundation for growth in every other part of your life.

Affirmation & Gratitude

I create harmony in my home, honouring it as my sanctuary and foundation of strength.

Taurus
26-March-2026

Taurus, today invites joy, playfulness, and creative expression. Your heart may feel lighter, encouraging you to pursue hobbies, romance, or anything that sparks laughter. Don't dismiss the importance of fun—when you allow yourself to play, your spirit is replenished. Romantic energy is also highlighted, whether you're deepening an existing bond or opening yourself to love. Creativity flows easily now, so use this time to bring colour and passion into your world. Joy isn't frivolous—it's essential for your well-being. Let your inner child lead the way.

Affirmation & Gratitude

I embrace joy, creativity, and love, trusting they enrich and uplift my spirit.

Taurus
27-March-2026

Health and daily routines are highlighted today, Taurus. You may feel motivated to organise your schedule, refine habits, or make small adjustments that support your well-being. Don't overload yourself; focus on simple, sustainable steps. Your body may send you signals now—listen to its needs, whether for rest, nourishment, or movement. Work responsibilities also benefit from methodical attention. The cosmos encourages balance today, reminding you that consistency is the key to resilience. By tending to your daily life with care, you build strength that supports your bigger goals.

Affirmation & Gratitude

I honour balance and consistency, knowing small daily steps create lasting well-being.

Taurus
28-March-2026

Taurus, relationships come into focus today. The stars encourage you to consider how balance plays out in your partnerships—romantic, platonic, or professional. Are you giving too much, or holding back when openness is needed? A conversation may help restore harmony if handled with patience and honesty. Don't fear vulnerability; authenticity builds stronger bonds. If single, pay attention to interactions that feel meaningful—new connections could carry long-term significance. Today is about creating relationships rooted in fairness, respect, and truth.

Affirmation & Gratitude

I welcome balance and honesty in my relationships, trusting authentic connections to grow stronger.

Taurus
29-March-2026

Deep emotions surface today, Taurus, as themes of intimacy, trust, and transformation are activated. You may find yourself reflecting on shared resources, finances, or hidden fears that influence your decisions. This is a powerful day to release what no longer serves—whether emotional baggage, unhealthy attachments, or outdated financial agreements. By leaning into vulnerability, you create space for renewal. Growth often comes through discomfort, but you have the patience and strength to move through it. Trust that letting go today opens the door to empowerment.

Affirmation & Gratitude

I release what no longer serves, trusting transformation to bring strength and clarity.

Taurus
30-March-2026

Optimism fills the air today, Taurus, as the cosmos encourages you to broaden your horizons. This could mean planning travel, exploring new ideas, or engaging in conversations that inspire growth. Your earthy nature values security, but today asks you to embrace curiosity. A learning opportunity may arise, or you may feel drawn to spiritual or philosophical exploration. Say yes to experiences that stretch your perspective—you'll find yourself enriched by what you discover. Expansion doesn't replace stability; it enhances it.

Affirmation & Gratitude

I embrace new horizons with courage, trusting curiosity to enrich my life.

Taurus
31-March-2026

Taurus, career matters and long-term ambitions are spotlighted today. Recognition for your steady efforts may appear, or you may be asked to step into a leadership role. While responsibility can feel heavy, remember that your persistence and patience are your strengths. Today is an ideal time to review your professional goals and ensure they align with your values. Practical steps taken now can build a lasting legacy. The universe is reminding you that success isn't about speed but about integrity and consistency.

Affirmation & Gratitude

I step forward with confidence, trusting persistence and integrity to build my legacy.

April
2026

Taurus
01-April-2026

Taurus, friendships and community ties are highlighted today. You may feel called to connect with like-minded people, share ideas, or participate in group activities that spark inspiration. Collaboration brings momentum now, but be discerning—some connections energise you while others drain. Gravitate toward people who share your values and goals. You may also find that teamwork helps you move forward on a project more quickly than you could alone. Trust your instincts about where to invest your loyalty. Today is about remembering you're stronger when surrounded by supportive energy.

Affirmation & Gratitude

I welcome friendships and communities that uplift, inspire, and align with my true values.

Taurus
02-April-2026

Taurus, today draws you inward toward introspection and reflection. You may crave solitude to process emotions or recharge your energy. This is not a day for pushing ahead but for listening to your intuition. Dreams, subtle signs, or synchronicities may offer important messages. Allow yourself space for journaling, meditation, or simply resting. By pausing, you prepare yourself for fresh starts on the horizon. Release old fears or burdens weighing you down. Stillness today is fertile ground for renewal and clarity.

Affirmation & Gratitude

I honour stillness and reflection, trusting quiet moments to restore strength and wisdom.

Taurus
03-April-2026

The Moon enters your sign today, Taurus, boosting your confidence and vitality. You may feel more visible, magnetic, and ready to embrace new beginnings. This is an excellent day for setting personal intentions, launching projects, or stepping into the spotlight. Others are drawn to your grounded presence, and opportunities may come because you're showing up authentically. Don't second-guess yourself—the stars are aligning to remind you of your worth. Today is about embodying self-assurance and taking steps that feel aligned with who you truly are becoming.

Affirmation & Gratitude

I shine with confidence, trusting authenticity to guide my steps and attract new opportunities.

Taurus
04-April-2026

Taurus, today shines a light on your resources—finances, possessions, and personal talents. You may feel motivated to review your budget, plan for long-term stability, or explore new ways of increasing income. But remember, abundance isn't only about money– it's also about valuing yourself and recognising your inner resources. Don't downplay your strengths; they are part of your wealth. Be practical, but also confident in your ability to create prosperity. A small decision today could shape your long-term security. Trust your steady approach.

Affirmation & Gratitude

I value my skills and trust my steady steps create lasting security and abundance.

Taurus
05-April-2026

Communication takes centre stage today, Taurus. Conversations may hold more weight than usual, offering clarity, inspiration, or even healing. Writing, teaching, or sharing your ideas is favoured now, as others listen to your grounded perspective. Keep an open mind—flexibility will help you see things differently and spark new insights. A short trip or an unexpected meeting could open fresh opportunities. Don't be afraid to express yourself honestly, but remember to listen carefully too. Balance in dialogue is key today.

Affirmation & Gratitude

I communicate with clarity and openness, trusting dialogue to bring insight and connection.

Taurus
06-April-2026

Taurus, your home and family life take focus today. You may feel called to nurture your living space, strengthen bonds with loved ones, or handle domestic responsibilities. Emotions may run deep, but your patience can restore harmony if conflicts arise. Creating peace at home helps ground you in every other part of your life. Small tasks like cooking, decluttering, or refreshing your space will lift your spirit. Honour your roots while also creating traditions that reflect who you are now.

Affirmation & Gratitude

I create harmony in my home, trusting it as the foundation for peace and strength.

Taurus
07-April-2026

Creativity and joy sparkle today, Taurus. You may feel inspired to explore hobbies, romance, or playful activities that bring colour to your world. The stars encourage you to lighten your heart and allow fun to flow, reminding you that joy is not a distraction but essential for balance. Romantic energy is heightened, so open your heart to connection and affection. Self-expression through art, music, or laughter heals your spirit now. Give yourself permission to shine in playful ways.

Affirmation & Gratitude

I embrace joy, creativity, and love, allowing playfulness to uplift and heal my spirit.

Taurus
08-April-2026

Taurus, your focus turns toward health, routines, and self-care today. The cosmos encourages you to refine your habits, making space for balance and long-term well-being. You may feel motivated to tidy your schedule, eat more mindfully, or address tasks you've been putting off. Don't overwhelm yourself—start with small, steady steps that feel achievable. If work feels demanding, approach it methodically rather than rushing. Remember, your strength lies in persistence, not speed. By prioritising your physical and emotional health today, you lay a foundation of stability that supports everything else.

Affirmation & Gratitude

I nurture my health and routines, trusting small, steady steps to bring balance and strength.

Taurus
09-April-2026

Relationships take centre stage today, Taurus. You may feel called to examine the give-and-take within your partnerships—whether romantic, professional, or friendships. Are you offering more than you're receiving, or holding back when openness is needed? Conversations may reveal truths, and though vulnerability can feel uncomfortable, it leads to greater trust and balance. The stars remind you that relationships flourish through authenticity, patience, and mutual respect. This is a good day to express your needs calmly and listen with care. Harmony is possible when both sides feel seen and valued.

Affirmation & Gratitude

I create balance in my relationships, trusting honesty and respect to deepen connections.

Taurus
10-April-2026

Taurus, today carries deep emotional intensity as matters of intimacy, trust, and shared resources come to the surface. You may feel prompted to face hidden fears or insecurities around love, money, or vulnerability. While it may feel uncomfortable, leaning into honesty and release opens the door to transformation. Financial discussions or reviews of commitments may also be highlighted—approach them with grounded practicality. Remember, renewal often comes from letting go of what no longer serves you. By embracing change, you discover new strength within yourself.

Affirmation & Gratitude

I release old fears and embrace transformation, trusting change to guide me toward strength and healing.

Taurus
11-April-2026

Optimism flows today, Taurus, as the cosmos invites you to broaden your horizons. You may feel inspired to explore learning, travel, or spiritual growth. A fresh perspective helps you see your life's bigger picture, reminding you not to get lost in details. Conversations with people from different backgrounds or exposure to new ideas could spark exciting insights. Your earthy energy craves stability, but today asks you to mix curiosity with grounded action. Opportunities for growth appear when you say yes to something new, even if it feels unfamiliar.

Affirmation & Gratitude

I embrace new horizons with courage, trusting exploration to enrich my journey.

Taurus
12-April-2026

Taurus, career and long-term goals are highlighted today. Recognition for your consistent efforts may come, or you may be called to take on a responsibility that showcases your reliability. While you might feel pressure, remember that persistence, not speed, is your strength. Today is also a good day for strategic planning—mapping out your ambitions for the months ahead. Align your goals with your values, and trust that small, steady steps will lead to long-term success. Your integrity is what sets you apart, and others are noticing.

Affirmation & Gratitude

I move steadily toward my goals, trusting persistence and integrity to shape my success.

Taurus
13-April-2026

Taurus, friendships and community connections come into focus. You may feel energised by working with others toward shared goals or inspired by conversations with like-minded people. A group project or gathering could bring fresh ideas. At the same time, you may notice which connections uplift you and which drain your energy. This is a good day to set boundaries while leaning into relationships that feel aligned. By surrounding yourself with positive, inspiring people, your dreams gain momentum. Collaboration opens doors you may not find alone.

Affirmation & Gratitude

I attract supportive friendships that inspire growth and joy in my life.

Taurus
14-April-2026

Reflection and rest call to you today, Taurus. You may crave solitude, preferring quiet activities that allow you to recharge. Dreams or intuition may deliver insights, so give yourself time to listen. If emotions surface, allow them to flow without judgement—this is part of your healing process. Rest isn't laziness; it is restoration, giving you the clarity needed for fresh beginnings ahead. Honour your need for peace today, and trust that by slowing down, you strengthen your resilience and wisdom for the future.

Affirmation & Gratitude

I honour stillness and reflection, trusting rest to restore my clarity and strength.

Taurus
15-April-2026

Taurus, the Moon lights up your sign today, boosting your energy, vitality, and visibility. You may feel more confident, ready to take bold steps, or eager to embrace a new chapter. This is an excellent day for setting personal intentions, starting a project, or simply showing up authentically. Others are drawn to your steady, grounded presence, and opportunities may appear simply because you're being yourself. Don't let self-doubt hold you back—the stars are reminding you that your unique gifts matter. Today is about shining brightly and claiming your space with grace and confidence.

Affirmation & Gratitude

I step confidently into my light, trusting my authenticity to guide my next steps.

Taurus
16-April-2026

Taurus, today brings focus to your resources—finances, possessions, and self-worth. You may feel prompted to review your budget, make practical plans, or explore new ways to create stability. Yet this energy also asks you to reflect on your inner resources—your talents, resilience, and steady determination. These are just as valuable as material wealth. Don't downplay your worth or skills; they are your foundation for abundance. A decision you make today could have long-lasting financial or personal benefits. Trust your ability to build prosperity through patience and persistence.

Affirmation & Gratitude

I value my worth and trust my steady steps to create lasting security and abundance.

Taurus
17-April-2026

Communication takes centre stage today, Taurus. You may find yourself in important conversations, writing, teaching, or sharing ideas that influence others. Your words carry weight now, so use them with care and clarity. Listen as much as you speak; insights come when you allow space for dialogue. A short trip, errand, or unexpected interaction could also bring inspiration. Stay curious and open-minded—rigid thinking blocks growth, but flexibility opens new possibilities. The universe is reminding you that wisdom often comes in small, everyday exchanges.

Affirmation & Gratitude

I communicate with clarity and openness, trusting meaningful conversations to bring insight and connection.

Taurus
18-April-2026

Taurus, your home and family life take the spotlight today. You may feel a strong urge to nurture your space, tend to domestic responsibilities, or connect with loved ones more deeply. Emotional conversations could arise, offering opportunities for understanding and healing. Creating comfort in your environment restores balance and strength in other areas of life. Even small actions—like tidying, cooking, or rearranging—refresh your energy. Honour both your roots and your evolving needs as you shape your home into a sanctuary that reflects your heart.

Affirmation & Gratitude

I create harmony in my home, honouring it as the foundation of peace and security.

Taurus
19-April-2026

Taurus, joy and creativity flow strongly today. The stars encourage you to embrace hobbies, romance, or playful experiences that uplift your spirit. Don't underestimate the healing power of fun—it restores energy that heavy responsibilities often drain. Allow your heart to open to love, whether through affection with a partner, quality time with friends, or self-expression in art, music, or writing. By giving yourself permission to enjoy life, you recharge your spirit. Joy isn't frivolous—it's nourishment for your soul. Let playfulness guide you today.

Affirmation & Gratitude

I embrace joy and creativity, allowing love and play to restore my energy.

Taurus
20-April-2026

Taurus, today highlights health, work, and daily balance. You may feel prompted to organise your schedule, refine habits, or prioritise your well-being. Don't aim for perfection—focus on steady, sustainable steps. If work demands your attention, approach it methodically, trusting your persistence to carry you through. Your body may also be asking for care—listen to its signals. Balance between productivity and rest is key. By creating structure today, you strengthen your resilience and build a solid foundation for future growth.

Affirmation & Gratitude

I honour my daily routines and create balance, trusting small steps to build strength and stability.

Taurus
21-April-2026

Relationships take centre stage today, Taurus. The stars encourage you to reflect on balance, fairness, and authenticity within your partnerships. Someone close may need more of your presence, but ensure your needs are also respected. A conversation may bring clarity if handled with patience and openness. If single, you may notice new opportunities for meaningful connection. Today reminds you that harmony is created not through perfection but through honesty and mutual respect. Authenticity deepens the bonds you truly value.

Affirmation & Gratitude

I welcome balanced and honest relationships, trusting authenticity to create deeper harmony.

Taurus
22-April-2026

Taurus, emotions run deep today as themes of intimacy, trust, and transformation come into focus. You may feel called to examine financial agreements, shared resources, or hidden fears that have been quietly shaping your choices. While intensity may arise, this is a chance to release what no longer serves you. Lean into vulnerability instead of resisting it—doing so strengthens your connections and allows for growth. Transformation is not always easy, but it leads to empowerment and renewal. Today, trust that letting go creates the space for something more aligned to arrive.

Affirmation & Gratitude

I release what no longer serves me, trusting transformation to bring renewal and strength.

Taurus
23-April-2026

Optimism returns today, Taurus, as the stars encourage you to broaden your horizons. You may feel inspired to explore new learning opportunities, plan travel, or engage in conversations that expand your worldview. Your earthy nature thrives on stability, but today asks you to weave in curiosity and adventure. Inspiration often comes when you step outside routine and see things from a different perspective. Say yes to something new, even if it feels unfamiliar. Growth now isn't about abandoning security—it's about blending it with exploration.

Affirmation & Gratitude

I embrace new horizons with curiosity, trusting learning and exploration to enrich my life.

Taurus
24-April-2026

Taurus, career and ambitions take the spotlight today. Recognition may come for your steady efforts, or you may be asked to take on more responsibility. While this could feel demanding, remember that persistence and reliability are your strengths. This is also a powerful day for long-term planning—look at where you want to be months or years from now and set practical steps to get there. Conversations with mentors or authority figures may open new doors, so approach them with calm confidence.

Affirmation & Gratitude

I step steadily toward my ambitions, trusting persistence and integrity to bring success.

Taurus
25-April-2026

Friendships and community ties are highlighted today, Taurus. You may feel energised by spending time with supportive people or collaborating on shared goals. A group project could gain momentum, or a social invitation may bring unexpected joy. However, you may also realise which connections no longer align with your energy. Be mindful of where you invest your loyalty and time—focus on those who uplift and inspire you. True friends encourage your growth and celebrate your steady strength. Today is about leaning into the connections that nourish you.

Affirmation & Gratitude

I attract friendships that inspire joy and growth, releasing those that no longer align.

Taurus
26-April-2026

Taurus, today invites you to pause, reflect, and recharge. You may feel less social and more drawn to solitude or introspective activities. This is a perfect day for journaling, meditating, or simply enjoying quiet moments that restore your spirit. Dreams or intuitive nudges may offer guidance, so pay attention to subtle signs. Don't view stillness as wasted time—it allows you to release burdens and strengthen clarity. By tending to your inner world now, you prepare yourself for the fresh beginnings ahead.

Affirmation & Gratitude

I honour stillness and reflection, trusting rest to renew my spirit and clarity.

Taurus
27-April-2026

The Moon enters your sign today, Taurus, bringing renewed energy, confidence, and visibility. You may feel motivated to set personal intentions, embrace fresh beginnings, or simply express yourself more authentically. Others notice your grounded presence, and opportunities may open because of it. This is a powerful day for starting new projects or taking bold steps that reflect who you truly are. Trust your steady strength and remind yourself that your authenticity is magnetic. Today is about stepping forward with grace and confidence.

Affirmation & Gratitude

I shine with confidence and embrace new beginnings, trusting authenticity to guide my path.

Taurus
28-April-2026

Taurus, your focus shifts to resources today—finances, possessions, and self-worth. You may feel motivated to create more stability, whether by budgeting, organising, or planning investments. Yet this is also a reminder that your true wealth lies in your inner resources—your patience, resilience, and skills. Be mindful not to compare yourself to others; your journey is uniquely yours. Practical steps you take today will build long-term prosperity. Abundance grows when you trust your worth and value your steady progress.

Affirmation & Gratitude

I value my worth and trust my steady actions to create lasting abundance.

Taurus
29-April-2026

Taurus, communication is highlighted today, and your words carry power. Conversations may reveal insights that shift your perspective or bring clarity to lingering issues. You may feel inspired to write, teach, or share your ideas with others—your grounded voice holds weight now. Short trips or errands could lead to chance encounters that spark inspiration. Be mindful of rigid thinking; remain open to fresh perspectives. The universe encourages curiosity today, reminding you that wisdom often arrives in unexpected places. Listen as much as you speak, and you'll discover deeper truths.

Affirmation & Gratitude

I communicate with clarity and openness, trusting dialogue to inspire growth and connection.

Taurus
30-April-2026

Home and family take centre stage today, Taurus. You may feel called to nurture your space, handle domestic responsibilities, or connect more deeply with loved ones. Emotional matters could surface, but your patience helps restore balance. Even small acts —like cooking a meal, decluttering, or refreshing your environment—bring peace and grounding. Family conversations may reveal important truths, offering opportunities for healing and connection. Remember, your home is not just walls—it's a sanctuary that reflects your inner stability. By creating harmony here, you strengthen every other area of your life.

Affirmation & Gratitude

I create harmony in my home, trusting it as the foundation of my strength and peace.

May 2026

Taurus
01-May-2026

Taurus, creativity and joy are alive within you today. You may feel drawn to hobbies, romance, or simply activities that make your spirit feel lighter. The stars encourage you to express yourself freely, whether through art, laughter, or affectionate connection. Don't downplay the importance of fun—joy replenishes your energy and keeps life in balance. Romantic energy flows, and playful conversations may deepen a bond. Allow yourself to be inspired, to colour outside the lines, and to live from the heart.

Affirmation & Gratitude

I embrace joy and creativity, trusting playfulness to uplift and restore my spirit.

Taurus
02-May-2026

Health and routines are in focus today, Taurus. You may feel motivated to refine your habits, organise your schedule, or address areas where life has slipped out of balance. Don't pressure yourself to do everything at once—focus on one or two steady changes. Your body may be sending signals; listen and respond with care. Work tasks benefit from your methodical approach, but don't forget to rest. Balance is key. By creating a routine that nurtures your body and spirit, you ensure long-term resilience and stability.

Affirmation & Gratitude

I honour balance in my routines, trusting small, steady steps to build lasting strength.

Taurus
03-May-2026

Relationships are highlighted today, Taurus, as the cosmos asks you to reflect on balance, fairness, and authenticity. Whether in love, friendship, or business, harmony comes through honesty and mutual respect. A conversation may feel necessary to clarify boundaries or deepen trust. If you're single, pay attention to new encounters—they may carry long-term significance. Don't shy away from vulnerability; true strength lies in openness. Today is about aligning your relationships with your values and making space for connections that nurture growth.

Affirmation & Gratitude

I create balanced, honest relationships, trusting authenticity to deepen my connections.

Taurus
04-May-2026

Taurus, deep emotions and transformative energy rise today. You may find yourself reflecting on intimacy, trust, or shared resources. Financial or emotional entanglements may require your attention. Though intensity can feel uncomfortable, it holds the key to renewal. The stars encourage you to release old fears or patterns that no longer serve you. By leaning into vulnerability and allowing yourself to grow, you step into empowerment. Transformation is not always easy, but it always brings strength. Trust the process—you're building resilience.

Affirmation & Gratitude

I embrace transformation, trusting release and renewal to guide me toward strength and clarity.

Taurus
05-May-2026

Taurus, optimism flows today as the stars invite you to broaden your perspective. This could come through travel planning, study, or conversations that inspire new ways of thinking. Your earthy energy prefers stability, but growth comes from curiosity and courage. Don't be afraid to say yes to opportunities that stretch your comfort zone. Whether it's exploring new ideas, trying something different, or connecting with diverse people, today supports expansion. Remember, you can keep your roots strong while letting your branches reach toward the sky.

Affirmation & Gratitude

I welcome new horizons with courage, trusting curiosity to enrich my journey.

Taurus
06-May-2026

Taurus, career and long-term ambitions are spotlighted today. You may be recognised for your steady contributions, or someone may turn to you for leadership. While responsibility might feel heavy, trust that you're prepared. This is a good day to revisit professional goals and ensure they align with your deeper values. Don't chase success for appearances—focus on what feels meaningful. Your persistence and patience are what set you apart, and others respect your grounded wisdom. Opportunities for advancement may come if you step forward with confidence.

Affirmation & Gratitude

I move confidently toward my goals, trusting patience and persistence to shape lasting success.

Taurus
07-May-2026

Friendships and community ties are highlighted, Taurus. Collaboration feels fruitful today, and a conversation with a like-minded person could inspire fresh ideas. A group project may gain traction, or you may notice support coming from your network when you least expect it. At the same time, you may feel called to let go of connections that no longer align with your values. Remember, your energy is precious—invest it in relationships that uplift you. The right people celebrate your growth and inspire you to keep going.

Affirmation & Gratitude

I attract friendships that uplift me, releasing connections that no longer align with my values.

Taurus
08-May-2026

Taurus, today draws you inward. You may crave quiet time, preferring solitude to social activity. This is an excellent day for journaling, meditating, or simply slowing down enough to listen to your inner voice. Your intuition is heightened now—pay attention to dreams, signs, or gut feelings. Emotional release may be part of the process; let it flow naturally. Rest isn't wasted—it's the pause that strengthens you for fresh beginnings. Honour your need for reflection and you'll find renewed clarity for the days ahead.

Affirmation & Gratitude

I honour stillness and solitude, trusting quiet moments to restore my clarity and strength.

Taurus
09-May-2026

The Moon lights up your sign today, Taurus, bringing confidence, vitality, and a sense of renewal. You may feel ready to start something fresh, take a bold step forward, or simply embody your authentic self more fully. Others are drawn to your calm strength and grounded energy, making this a perfect day for visibility. Trust yourself and don't let doubts hold you back. Set intentions that feel aligned with your true desires, and know that your presence alone creates opportunities.

Affirmation & Gratitude

I shine with authenticity and confidence, trusting my steady nature to guide my steps.

Taurus
10-May-2026

Taurus, today your attention turns to finances, resources, and self-worth. You may feel prompted to organise money matters, review budgets, or explore new ways to build stability. This is also about valuing your inner resources—your skills, determination, and resilience. Don't underestimate your gifts; they are the foundation of abundance. Avoid comparison with others, as it distracts from your unique path. Small, practical steps you take today can lead to lasting prosperity. Trust that your steady approach creates solid results.

Affirmation & Gratitude

I value my worth and trust my steady steps to create prosperity and security.

Taurus
11-May-2026

Communication is in the spotlight today, Taurus. Conversations may bring clarity, or you may feel inspired to share your ideas more openly. Writing, teaching, or studying is favoured, as your grounded perspective resonates with others. A short trip or unexpected exchange could spark inspiration. Be flexible in your thinking—new perspectives can open doors. Listen as much as you speak; meaningful insights come when you remain curious. Today is about using your voice with honesty while staying open to learning from others.

Affirmation & Gratitude

I communicate with clarity and openness, trusting dialogue to inspire growth.

Taurus
12-May-2026

Taurus, your home and family life take precedence today. You may feel a need to nurture your space, handle domestic responsibilities, or connect more deeply with loved ones. Emotions may surface, and though conversations could feel intense, they also hold the potential for healing. Creating peace at home strengthens your sense of security and stability. Even simple actions—like tidying, cooking, or refreshing your space—help restore balance. Honour your roots while also shaping traditions that reflect your growth.

Affirmation & Gratitude

I create peace and balance in my home, honouring it as my sanctuary and foundation.

Taurus
13-May-2026

Taurus, today highlights creativity, romance, and joy. You may feel drawn to hobbies, art, or playful activities that lighten your spirit. Romantic energy is strong—conversations or gestures of affection could deepen bonds. If you've been too focused on responsibilities, today reminds you that joy is a vital part of balance. Allow yourself to explore beauty, laughter, and connection without guilt. Self-expression, whether through music, words, or simply laughter with loved ones, nourishes your soul. Today is about celebrating life's sweeter moments and remembering they are just as important as hard work.

Affirmation & Gratitude

I embrace joy and creativity, trusting playfulness to restore balance and uplift my spirit.

Taurus
14-May-2026

Health, routines, and balance are in focus today, Taurus. You may feel motivated to refine daily habits or create structure where things have become chaotic. This isn't about perfection—it's about small, steady improvements that build resilience over time. Your body may signal what it needs—listen carefully, whether it's rest, nourishment, or gentle movement. Work tasks can be handled with patience and method, but don't let them overwhelm you. Today supports creating harmony between productivity and well-being. Grounding routines now set you up for long-term stability and peace.

Affirmation & Gratitude

I honour balance in my routines, trusting small, steady steps to strengthen my body and mind.

Taurus
15-May-2026

Taurus, relationships take centre stage today. Whether in romance, friendship, or business, you're encouraged to reflect on balance, fairness, and authenticity. A conversation may bring clarity or reveal where adjustments are needed. Don't shy away from vulnerability; being open deepens trust. If single, new connections may surface that carry potential for meaningful bonds. Remember, harmony doesn't mean avoiding conflict—it means facing challenges with patience and honesty. By showing up authentically, you attract relationships that align with your true values and support your growth.

Affirmation & Gratitude

I welcome balanced and authentic connections, trusting honesty to strengthen my relationships.

Taurus
16-May-2026

Taurus, today invites deep reflection on trust, intimacy, and transformation. You may feel called to review shared resources, financial commitments, or emotional bonds. Old fears or insecurities could surface, but they're showing you where growth is needed. This is an opportunity to release what no longer serves, creating space for renewal. Transformation isn't always comfortable, but it clears away what blocks your path. By leaning into vulnerability and honesty, you discover new strength. Healing is possible now if you're willing to embrace change.

Affirmation & Gratitude

I release what no longer serves me, trusting transformation to guide me toward strength and clarity.

Taurus
17-May-2026

Expansion and optimism fill the day, Taurus. You may feel inspired to learn, explore, or open yourself to new experiences. Conversations with others could spark exciting insights, or you might feel drawn to study or plan travel. Your earthy energy seeks security, but today the stars remind you that growth comes when you stretch beyond the familiar. Balance curiosity with practicality, and you'll find opportunities that both inspire and sustain you. Allow yourself to say yes to something new—you're ready for expansion.

Affirmation & Gratitude

I embrace growth and curiosity, trusting new experiences to enrich my life.

Taurus
18-May-2026

Taurus, career and long-term goals take focus today. Recognition for your steady efforts may arrive, or you could be asked to step into a leadership role. This is a powerful day for planning and strategy—look at your bigger picture and align your goals with your values. Your persistence and patience are admired, and doors may open because of them. Don't underestimate the influence of your grounded nature; it sets you apart in a world often chasing quick wins. Today supports lasting progress built step by steady step.

Affirmation & Gratitude

I step confidently toward my ambitions, trusting patience and persistence to shape my success.

Taurus
19-May-2026

Friendships, teamwork, and community energy surround you today, Taurus. You may feel inspired to collaborate, join forces, or share ideas with others. A group project could gain momentum, or you may discover new opportunities through your social networks. This is also a day to reflect on which connections energise you and which drain your spirit. Invest your time where you feel supported and celebrated. Surrounding yourself with like-minded people helps your dreams take root and grow stronger.

Affirmation & Gratitude

I welcome supportive connections, trusting collaboration and community to strengthen my path.

Taurus
20-May-2026

Taurus, today calls for rest, reflection, and spiritual renewal. You may feel less social and more introspective, drawn to journaling, meditation, or simply quiet moments with yourself. The cosmos encourages you to process emotions that have been lingering under the surface—acknowledge them, then release. Pay attention to dreams or subtle synchronicities; they carry guidance now. Don't see stillness as wasted time—this pause is your reset before fresh energy arrives. Healing happens in silence, and by leaning into it, you strengthen your inner wisdom.

Affirmation & Gratitude

I honour stillness and reflection, trusting quiet moments to bring healing and clarity.

Taurus
21-May-2026

The Sun enters Gemini today, Taurus, shifting your focus toward finances, self-worth, and personal resources. This month highlights your relationship with money, but also the way you value your time, energy, and skills. You may feel prompted to organise your budget, plan for long-term security, or find new ways to increase income. Don't overlook the abundance you already carry—your resilience and persistence are forms of wealth too. Today marks a fresh start in creating stability by aligning your values with your practical goals.

Affirmation & Gratitude

I value my worth and trust my steady steps to create lasting abundance.

Taurus
22-May-2026

Communication is highlighted today, Taurus. Conversations may bring clarity, healing, or inspiration, provided you're willing to stay open-minded. Writing, teaching, or sharing your ideas flows more easily now, and others may be drawn to your grounded perspective. Be mindful of rigid thinking—flexibility is the key to unlocking new insights. Short trips, errands, or unexpected encounters could offer opportunities you hadn't considered. The stars remind you that curiosity is your ally today—allow yourself to see things from fresh angles.

Affirmation & Gratitude

I communicate with clarity and openness, trusting dialogue to inspire growth and understanding.

Taurus
23-May-2026

Taurus, your home and family life are highlighted today. You may feel pulled to nurture your environment, tidy your space, or connect with loved ones in meaningful ways. Conversations with family may bring up emotions, but they also hold the potential for healing if approached with patience. Even small gestures—like sharing a meal or refreshing your home—restore balance. Your home is your sanctuary, and when it feels peaceful, it supports every other part of your life. Today, focus on grounding yourself in that foundation.

Affirmation & Gratitude

I create harmony in my home, trusting it as the foundation of peace and security.

Taurus
24-May-2026

Joy and creativity come alive today, Taurus. The cosmos encourages you to embrace hobbies, play, and romance. Don't dismiss fun as unimportant—joy is essential for balance and renewal. Whether you're exploring art, enjoying laughter with loved ones, or deepening a romantic bond, today offers a chance to reconnect with your heart. Your playful energy is magnetic, drawing others toward you. Remember, self-expression is not frivolous—it's healing. Allow yourself to explore life's beauty and delight in small pleasures.

Affirmation & Gratitude

I embrace joy and creativity, trusting play and laughter to nourish my spirit.

Taurus
25-May-2026

Taurus, today brings focus to health, routines, and organisation. You may feel motivated to make practical adjustments to your daily life—refining habits, tackling tasks, or creating balance between work and rest. Don't overwhelm yourself by doing everything at once; steady steps are more sustainable. Your body may be asking for care now—listen and respond with kindness. Productivity flows more easily when it's balanced with self-care. Today supports building structure that will serve you long term.

Affirmation & Gratitude

I honour balance in my routines, trusting small, consistent steps to strengthen my foundation.

Taurus
26-May-2026

Relationships take centre stage today, Taurus. The stars ask you to reflect on balance, fairness, and openness in your partnerships. Are you giving too much, or holding back when your heart wants to share? A conversation may bring clarity if handled with patience and honesty. If single, you may notice new opportunities for connection that feel aligned with your values. Authenticity is key—relationships rooted in truth flourish now. This is a day to honour your needs while respecting others'.

Affirmation & Gratitude

I welcome balanced and authentic relationships, trusting honesty to deepen connection.

Taurus
27-May-2026

Taurus, today highlights themes of intimacy, vulnerability, and transformation. You may find yourself reflecting on deeper emotional bonds or financial matters tied to shared resources. Something hidden could surface, urging you to confront fears or insecurities you've avoided. Though this may feel intense, it's also empowering—the universe is asking you to release what no longer serves. Transformation requires courage, but you already carry the steady patience to see it through. Allow yourself to lean into honesty and trust, and you'll find renewal.

Affirmation & Gratitude

I release what no longer serves, trusting transformation to guide me toward strength and clarity.

Taurus
28-May-2026

Optimism and expansion guide you today, Taurus. You may feel inspired to learn, explore, or broaden your perspective through study, travel, or conversation. Your earthy energy often craves stability, but today the stars ask you to stretch beyond the familiar. New opportunities may come through people from different backgrounds or fresh philosophies that spark your curiosity. Growth doesn't mean abandoning security—it means blending it with exploration. By opening your mind, you enrich your journey and find fresh excitement in the path ahead.

Affirmation & Gratitude

I embrace new horizons with courage, trusting curiosity to enrich my life.

Taurus
29-May-2026

Taurus, career and long-term ambitions are spotlighted today. Recognition may come for your persistence, or you may be called to step into a role that requires responsibility and leadership. While pressure may feel heavy, your reliability and grounded nature are your strengths. This is an excellent day to plan strategically, aligning your goals with your values. Don't chase quick wins—focus on building a foundation that lasts. Trust that your persistence will be rewarded. Opportunities may arise if you show up with confidence and integrity.

Affirmation & Gratitude

I move steadily toward my goals, trusting persistence and patience to shape lasting success.

Taurus
30-May-2026

Friendships, teamwork, and community energy are highlighted today, Taurus. You may feel energised by collaboration or inspired by conversations with supportive people. A group project may take shape, or you could find encouragement from like minded souls who share your vision. At the same time, you may recognise connections that no longer align. Focus your energy where you feel uplifted and valued. Remember, your loyalty is precious—invest it wisely. Surrounding yourself with positive influences strengthens your dreams and brings momentum.

Affirmation & Gratitude

I attract supportive friendships and collaborations that inspire growth and joy.

Taurus
31-May-2026

Taurus, today invites rest, reflection, and emotional release. You may feel quieter than usual, preferring solitude over social activity. Use this time to recharge and listen to your inner voice. Intuition is strong now, and dreams or subtle signs could offer important guidance. Don't see stillness as unproductive—this is a healing pause that clears space for fresh beginnings. Allow yourself to let go of past burdens. By honouring rest, you renew your energy and prepare for the days ahead.

Affirmation & Gratitude

I honour stillness and rest, trusting reflection to bring peace and clarity.

June 2026

Taurus
01-June-2026

The Moon enters your sign today, Taurus, bringing renewed energy, confidence, and vitality. You may feel ready to start fresh projects, express yourself more openly, or step into the spotlight. Others are drawn to your calm strength, and opportunities may come simply because of your authentic presence. This is a perfect day to set personal intentions, embrace new beginnings, and take steps that reflect your values. Trust yourself—you don't need to rush; your steady pace is enough.

Affirmation & Gratitude

I shine with authenticity, stepping forward confidently into new beginnings.

Taurus
02-June-2026

Taurus, today highlights your finances, possessions, and sense of self-worth. You may feel motivated to organise budgets, review spending, or explore new ways of building stability. The stars remind you that true abundance isn't only financial—it's also your patience, persistence, and talents. Don't undervalue yourself or compare your journey to others. A small, practical decision made today could have long-term benefits. Trust that steady progress will lead to prosperity, provided you align your actions with your values.

Affirmation & Gratitude

I value my worth and trust my steady actions to build lasting security.

Taurus
03-June-2026

Taurus, communication is spotlighted today, making it a powerful time to express your ideas or engage in meaningful dialogue. You may find yourself writing, teaching, or sharing your perspective in a way that resonates with others. Conversations could lead to fresh insights or solutions to lingering issues. Be open-minded—sometimes wisdom comes from unexpected sources. A short trip, errand, or spontaneous meeting may open new doors. Your grounded presence helps you speak with clarity and authority, but flexibility allows you to learn just as much as you share.

Affirmation & Gratitude

I communicate with clarity and openness, trusting meaningful dialogue to bring insight and growth.

Taurus
04-June-2026

Taurus, your home and family life come into focus today. You may feel the need to nurture your space, strengthen bonds, or handle domestic responsibilities. Emotional conversations may arise, offering opportunities for understanding and healing if handled with patience. Even simple acts—like cooking, cleaning, or rearranging furniture—can restore peace and grounding. Your home reflects your inner stability, so tending to it strengthens your sense of security. Today is about creating harmony in your personal world so you can move forward with balance and calm.

Affirmation & Gratitude

I create peace and balance in my home, honouring it as my sanctuary.

Taurus
05-June-2026

Joy and creativity sparkle today, Taurus. The cosmos encourages you to step away from routine and allow yourself to play, laugh, and express your passions. Romance is also favoured, with opportunities for deeper connection through affection and lightheartedness. Hobbies or creative pursuits bring healing and inspiration now, reminding you that life isn't only about duty—it's also about joy. Your magnetic energy is amplified when you embrace your playful side, attracting both people and opportunities that resonate with your heart. Today, celebrate the beauty of living fully.

Affirmation & Gratitude

I embrace joy and creativity, trusting play and love to nourish my spirit.

Taurus
06-June-2026

Taurus, health, routines, and balance are in focus today. You may feel motivated to refine habits, get organised, or address tasks that have been lingering. Don't overwhelm yourself—small, steady steps are more effective than drastic changes. Listen to your body's needs; rest if tired, move if restless, nourish if depleted. At work, your methodical approach helps you manage responsibilities efficiently. Today supports creating stability through structure and consistency, reminding you that long-term resilience comes from daily practices.

Affirmation & Gratitude

I honour balance in my routines, trusting small, consistent steps to build strength.

Taurus
07-June-2026

Relationships are highlighted today, Taurus. Whether in love, friendship, or business, you're asked to reflect on balance, reciprocity, and authenticity. Someone close may seek your support, but ensure your own needs are respected too. A heartfelt conversation could clear the air or strengthen trust. If single, new connections may carry meaningful potential. Don't fear vulnerability—it's the bridge to deeper bonds. Harmony doesn't come from avoiding conflict but from facing it with honesty and patience.

Affirmation & Gratitude

I welcome balanced, authentic relationships, trusting honesty to deepen connections.

Taurus
08-June-2026

Deep transformation energy surrounds you today, Taurus. Matters of intimacy, shared resources, or trust may rise to the surface. Financial discussions may need attention, or emotions may call for release. While this intensity could feel uncomfortable, it carries the gift of renewal. By letting go of fears or outdated attachments, you create space for growth and empowerment. Transformation is part of life's rhythm, and you're ready to embrace it with steady courage. Today is about trusting that release makes room for something stronger.

Affirmation & Gratitude

I embrace transformation, trusting release and renewal to strengthen me.

Taurus
09-June-2026

Taurus, optimism and expansion fill the air today. The stars encourage you to broaden your perspective through study, travel planning, or simply exploring new ideas. Your earthy nature values stability, but growth happens when you say yes to experiences beyond your comfort zone. Conversations with people from different walks of life may spark inspiration. Allow curiosity to guide you—the bigger picture becomes clearer when you step back from details. Today, balance your steady roots with adventurous branches.

Affirmation & Gratitude

I welcome growth and curiosity, trusting new horizons to enrich my journey.

Taurus
10-June-2026

Taurus, today shines a spotlight on your career and long-term ambitions. You may feel recognition for your consistent efforts or be offered new responsibilities that require your steady hand. While this could feel like added pressure, your reliability and patience set you apart. Use today to review your goals—are they aligned with your values? Success isn't just about achievement; it's about building something meaningful that lasts. Practical planning is favoured, and conversations with mentors or authority figures may open new doors.

Affirmation & Gratitude

I step steadily toward my ambitions, trusting patience and persistence to shape my legacy.

Taurus
11-June-2026

Friendships and community ties are highlighted, Taurus. You may feel inspired to connect with like-minded people, collaborate on shared projects, or revisit group goals. Social energy is strong, and you could find joy in gatherings or conversations that spark inspiration. Be mindful of which connections energise you and which leave you drained. Your loyalty is precious—invest it where it feels reciprocated. By surrounding yourself with supportive people, you create momentum toward your dreams and strengthen your confidence in your path.

Affirmation & Gratitude

I welcome friendships that uplift me and invest my energy where I feel supported and inspired.

Taurus
12-June-2026

Taurus, today invites reflection, solitude, and emotional release. You may crave quiet moments away from the noise, giving yourself space to recharge. Your intuition is heightened—pay attention to subtle signs, dreams, or inner whispers that guide you. Old worries or burdens may resurface; acknowledge them and gently let them go. Stillness restores clarity and prepares you for the new beginnings ahead. Don't view rest as laziness—it's an essential part of your growth. Today is about listening deeply to your inner self.

Affirmation & Gratitude

I honour stillness and rest, trusting reflection to bring healing and renewal.

Taurus
13-June-2026

The Moon enters your sign today, Taurus, boosting confidence, vitality, and visibility. You may feel ready to set personal intentions, launch projects, or express yourself more authentically. Others notice your calm strength and grounded presence, making this an ideal day to take bold steps forward. Trust yourself—you don't need to rush or compare. Your steady nature is enough, and opportunities are drawn to your authenticity. This is your moment to claim space with grace, showing the world who you truly are.

Affirmation & Gratitude

I shine with authenticity, trusting my steady strength to guide new beginnings.

Taurus
14-June-2026

Taurus, resources and self-worth are in focus today. You may feel called to review your finances, organise possessions, or explore new ways of building security. But this is also about recognising the abundance within you—your skills, patience, and resilience are invaluable. Avoid comparing your progress with others; your path is uniquely your own. A small, practical decision today may have lasting benefits. Trust your ability to build prosperity step by step. The universe rewards consistency, and you excel at that.

Affirmation & Gratitude

I value my worth and trust my steady steps to create lasting abundance.

Taurus
15-June-2026

Communication is spotlighted, Taurus. Conversations today carry weight, whether personal or professional, and could lead to new opportunities or clarity on an issue. You may feel drawn to share your ideas through writing, teaching, or speaking, and others will appreciate your calm, grounded approach. Be flexible in your thinking and willing to listen as much as you speak. Short trips or unexpected encounters may spark inspiration. The stars remind you that wisdom often comes through everyday exchanges.

Affirmation & Gratitude

I communicate with clarity and openness, trusting dialogue to inspire insight and growth.

Taurus
16-June-2026

Taurus, home and family matters take priority today. You may feel pulled to nurture your space, handle domestic responsibilities, or connect more deeply with loved ones. Emotional conversations could arise, but your patience and steadiness can help resolve misunderstandings. Even simple actions—like cooking, decluttering, or refreshing a room—can restore comfort and grounding. Your home is your sanctuary, and when it feels balanced, you feel supported in all other areas of life. Focus today on strengthening that foundation of peace.

Affirmation & Gratitude

I create harmony in my home, honouring it as the foundation of my strength and peace.

Taurus
17-June-2026

Taurus, creativity and joy take centre stage today. The stars encourage you to reconnect with your playful side through hobbies, art, or romance. If life has felt heavy, today offers a chance to lighten your spirit and remember that joy is a powerful form of healing. Romantic connections deepen through laughter and shared experiences, while solo pursuits allow you to express your inner beauty. Don't dismiss fun as unimportant—it restores balance and gives you strength to tackle responsibilities. Let your heart guide you toward experiences that uplift and inspire.

Affirmation & Gratitude

I embrace joy and creativity, trusting playfulness to nourish my heart and spirit.

Taurus
18-June-2026

Health and routines are highlighted, Taurus. You may feel motivated to refine daily habits, organise responsibilities, or care for your body more intentionally. Don't push yourself to achieve everything at once; small, steady steps are what create real change. The stars remind you that your body is your vessel—listen to what it needs. Whether it's rest, nourishment, or gentle movement, honouring yourself now will restore balance. Work tasks can be handled methodically today, but avoid overcommitting. Simplicity and balance bring the best results.

Affirmation & Gratitude

I nurture myself with balance, trusting small, steady actions to strengthen my body and spirit.

Taurus
19-June-2026

Taurus, relationships move into the spotlight. The cosmos asks you to reflect on how you show up in partnerships and what balance looks like for you. A partner, friend, or colleague may seek clarity or support, but ensure your needs are also respected. Conversations may feel vulnerable but can lead to deeper trust. If single, notice new encounters that feel aligned with your values. Harmony is created when both sides feel seen and valued. Today is about giving and receiving love in equal measure.

Affirmation & Gratitude

I honour balance in my relationships, trusting honesty and respect to deepen connections.

Taurus
20-June-2026

Transformation energy surrounds you today, Taurus. Matters of intimacy, shared resources, or deeper emotions may come to the surface. You may feel called to release fears, patterns, or attachments that no longer support your growth. While this process can feel intense, it brings renewal and empowerment. Financially, joint commitments may need review—approach them with honesty. Emotionally, lean into vulnerability, as it opens the door to healing. Trust that change, though sometimes uncomfortable, creates space for strength and clarity.

Affirmation & Gratitude

I release what no longer serves, trusting transformation to guide me into renewal and empowerment.

Taurus
21-June-2026

The Solstice arrives today, Taurus, with the Sun entering Cancer. This shift highlights communication, learning, and the way you share your thoughts with others. You may feel inspired to write, study, or connect more meaningfully through dialogue. Conversations carry extra significance now—be mindful of your words, as they can uplift or discourage. The next month encourages growth through curiosity and exchange. Say yes to new ideas or short journeys that expand your perspective. This is a season for connection, learning, and clarity.

Affirmation & Gratitude

I communicate with clarity and openness, trusting curiosity to expand my understanding.

Taurus
22-June-2026

Taurus, your home and family take focus today. The stars encourage you to create harmony within your private world, whether through nurturing relationships, handling domestic responsibilities, or refreshing your living space. Emotional conversations may arise, but your grounded presence can ease tension and restore balance. Even small actions like cleaning, cooking, or adding beauty to your space make a difference. When your home feels peaceful, you feel supported in everything else you do. Today is about strengthening your sanctuary.

Affirmation & Gratitude

I create peace and stability in my home, trusting it as the foundation of my strength.

Taurus
23-June-2026

Joy and creativity flow today, Taurus. You may feel inspired to explore hobbies, romance, or simply let your playful spirit shine. The universe reminds you that joy is not frivolous—it's vital. Your energy feels magnetic, drawing others toward you when you embrace laughter and love. Romantic connections flourish, while creative projects may surprise you with inspiration. Allow your inner child to guide your day. By reconnecting with lightheartedness, you recharge your energy and strengthen your spirit for the days ahead.

Affirmation & Gratitude

I embrace joy and play, trusting creativity and laughter to uplift and restore me.

Taurus
24-June-2026

Taurus, health, routines, and daily organisation are emphasised today. You may feel motivated to refine your schedule, clear clutter, or address responsibilities you've been putting off. This is not about perfection, but about creating consistency that supports your long-term stability. Your body may also ask for attention—listen to its signals and respond with care. By balancing productivity with rest, you strengthen your resilience. The cosmos supports practical adjustments that bring peace of mind, leaving you with a sense of control and accomplishment.

Affirmation & Gratitude

I honour balance in my daily life, trusting steady steps to bring me strength and clarity.

Taurus
25-June-2026

Relationships are highlighted today, Taurus. The cosmos invites you to examine fairness, trust, and reciprocity in your partnerships. Whether in love, friendship, or business, harmony requires openness and balance. Conversations may feel necessary to realign expectations or clarify boundaries. If you're single, the energy supports meeting someone who resonates with your values. Authenticity is your guide—don't settle for connections that don't feel genuine. Today is about showing up honestly and expecting the same in return.

Affirmation & Gratitude

I welcome balanced, authentic relationships, trusting honesty and openness to strengthen my bonds.

Taurus
26-June-2026

Taurus, deep emotional themes rise to the surface today. Matters of intimacy, trust, and shared resources may require your attention. This could feel intense, but it carries the potential for healing and transformation. Don't shy away from vulnerability by facing hidden fears or insecurities, you create space for growth. Financially, joint commitments may need review. Spiritually, this is a day to release what weighs you down, knowing renewal follows release. Trust that transformation, though sometimes uncomfortable, strengthens your foundation for the future.

Affirmation & Gratitude

I release what no longer serves me, trusting transformation to bring renewal and strength.

Taurus
27-June-2026

Optimism and expansion fill your world today, Taurus. You may feel inspired to learn something new, explore different perspectives, or plan an adventure. The stars encourage you to step outside routine and embrace curiosity. Conversations with people from different walks of life may open doors, and inspiration may come from unexpected sources. Your earthy energy thrives on security, but today reminds you that growth happens when you stretch beyond the familiar. Balance your need for stability with your desire for exploration.

Affirmation & Gratitude

I welcome growth and curiosity, trusting new experiences to enrich my path.

Taurus
28-June-2026

Taurus, career and long-term ambitions are spotlighted. Recognition for your hard work may arrive, or you may be asked to take on a leadership role. While responsibility could feel heavy, your persistence and reliability are your strengths. Use today to clarify your professional goals and ensure they align with your values. Avoid chasing quick results—instead, focus on creating lasting progress. Your grounded energy inspires confidence in others, and opportunities may arise because of it. Trust your steady approach.

Affirmation & Gratitude

I move confidently toward my goals, trusting persistence and integrity to create success.

Taurus
29-June-2026

Taurus, friendships and community ties are highlighted today. You may feel uplifted by connecting with supportive people or collaborating on group goals. Conversations could spark inspiration, helping you see new possibilities. At the same time, you may notice which connections no longer align with your energy. Invest your loyalty where you feel valued and celebrated. By surrounding yourself with people who encourage growth, you create momentum for your dreams. Social energy feels strong today—lean into it.

Affirmation & Gratitude

I attract friendships that inspire growth, joy, and mutual support.

Taurus
30-June-2026

Reflection and rest take focus today, Taurus. You may feel quieter, preferring solitude to social activity. Use this time to recharge, process recent events, or listen to your intuition. Dreams or subtle signs may carry important guidance now. This is not a day for pushing forward, but for releasing what's no longer needed. Honour stillness and allow it to strengthen your clarity. By resting today, you prepare for the new beginnings waiting just around the corner.

Affirmation & Gratitude

I honour stillness and solitude, trusting reflection to restore my peace and wisdom.

July 2026

Taurus
01-July-2026

Taurus, the Moon enters your sign today, bringing fresh energy, confidence, and visibility. You may feel ready to start a new project, embrace a bold decision, or simply express yourself more authentically. Others are drawn to your grounded presence, and opportunities may arise because of it. This is a powerful day for setting intentions and aligning them with your values. Don't let self-doubt creep in—you are stronger than you realise. Your steady, calm nature is magnetic, and when you trust yourself, the universe responds in kind.

Affirmation & Gratitude

I shine with authenticity and step forward with confidence, trusting my steady nature to guide me.

Taurus
02-July-2026

Taurus, today highlights your finances, possessions, and sense of self-worth. You may feel prompted to organise budgets, review spending, or explore new opportunities to create security. But this isn't only about material wealth—it's also about valuing yourself. Don't underestimate the power of your resilience, patience, and talents. They are your true foundation for abundance. A small, practical step you take today could bring long-term stability. Avoid comparing yourself to others; your journey is uniquely your own.

Affirmation & Gratitude

I value my worth and trust my steady steps to build lasting prosperity.

Taurus
03-July-2026

Communication is at the forefront today, Taurus. Important conversations may arise, offering clarity or inspiration. You may also feel drawn to writing, teaching, or sharing your ideas in some form. Be mindful of your words, as they carry influence now. Listen carefully as well—insightful messages may come from unexpected places. Short trips or errands could also bring fresh perspectives. Flexibility is key today; staying open allows wisdom to flow more freely. Trust your ability to communicate with grounded clarity and patience.

Affirmation & Gratitude

I communicate with clarity and openness, trusting dialogue to inspire growth.

Taurus
04-July-2026

Home and family take priority today, Taurus. You may feel called to nurture your environment, handle domestic responsibilities, or connect more deeply with loved ones. Conversations with family could reveal opportunities for understanding and healing. Even small tasks—like tidying, cooking, or refreshing your space—help create harmony. Your home is your sanctuary, and when it feels peaceful, you feel stronger in every other area of life. Focus today on strengthening your roots while also honouring the growth you've achieved.

Affirmation & Gratitude

I create peace and stability in my home, honouring it as my foundation of strength.

Taurus
05-July-2026

Creativity and joy sparkle today, Taurus. The cosmos encourages you to step away from seriousness and embrace hobbies, romance, and play. Express yourself freely through music, art, or laughter—it restores your spirit and reminds you that joy is vital, not optional. Romantic energy flows easily, bringing warmth to relationships. Your playful nature is magnetic now, attracting positive energy and fresh inspiration. Let your inner child lead the way, and don't be afraid to indulge in beauty and fun.

Affirmation & Gratitude

I embrace joy and creativity, trusting playfulness to uplift and heal my spirit.

Taurus
06-July-2026

Taurus, today highlights your health, routines, and work-life balance. You may feel motivated to refine your schedule, organise tasks, or focus on your body's needs. Consistency is your strength, so aim for steady improvements instead of dramatic changes. Your grounded approach helps you manage responsibilities efficiently while still leaving time for rest. The stars remind you that caring for yourself is the foundation of productivity and resilience. Today supports small, practical steps that improve your well-being long term.

Affirmation & Gratitude

I honour balance in my routines, trusting steady habits to build strength and stability.

Taurus
07-July-2026

Relationships are spotlighted today, Taurus. The stars ask you to reflect on fairness, balance, and authenticity in your partnerships. Someone close may need your presence, but make sure your own needs are respected as well. A heartfelt conversation could bring greater understanding and deepen trust. If single, pay attention to new connections—they may carry long-term significance. Today encourages vulnerability and openness, reminding you that genuine harmony is built on honesty and respect.

Affirmation & Gratitude

I welcome balanced and authentic relationships, trusting honesty to deepen my connections.

Taurus
08-July-2026

Taurus, today's cosmic energy turns your focus inward toward intimacy, trust, and transformation. Matters related to shared resources, financial partnerships, or deeper emotional connections may come up. You may be asked to release fears or insecurities that have been holding you back. Vulnerability may feel uncomfortable, but it leads to healing and growth. This is also a good day to review financial agreements and ensure they reflect your values. By letting go of what no longer serves, you open space for renewal and empowerment.

Affirmation & Gratitude

I release fears and welcome transformation, trusting vulnerability to strengthen my heart and spirit.

Taurus
09-July-2026

Optimism and curiosity expand your world today, Taurus. You may feel drawn to new experiences—whether through study, travel, or meaningful conversations that broaden your perspective. The universe is reminding you that growth doesn't mean abandoning stability; it means blending your steady nature with openness to exploration. Someone from a different background may inspire you with fresh ideas. Say yes to learning something new, even if it feels outside your usual comfort zone. Today encourages you to embrace adventure with trust in your grounded strength.

Affirmation & Gratitude

I welcome growth and exploration, trusting curiosity to enrich my journey.

Taurus
10-July-2026

Taurus, career and ambitions are in the spotlight today. Recognition may arrive for your persistence, or you may be asked to step into greater responsibility. While pressure might feel heavy, your grounded nature helps you handle it with grace. Today is also perfect for reviewing your long-term goals and aligning them with your values. Practical planning now sets you up for future success. Remember, success isn't about rushing—it's about steady progress that creates lasting results. Trust the legacy you are building one step at a time.

Affirmation & Gratitude

I step steadily toward my ambitions, trusting patience and persistence to shape my legacy.

Taurus
11-July-2026

Friendships and social connections are highlighted today, Taurus. The cosmos encourages collaboration and community involvement. A group project may gather momentum, or you could be inspired by conversations with people who share your vision. This is also a good day to reflect on who truly supports you and who no longer aligns with your path. Invest your loyalty in those who energise and uplift you. By surrounding yourself with positive influences, you give your dreams the strength to grow.

Affirmation & Gratitude

I welcome supportive friendships, trusting collaboration to inspire my growth and joy.

Taurus
12-July-2026

Taurus, today invites introspection and rest. You may feel quieter than usual, seeking time alone to recharge. This is an excellent day for journaling, meditation, or connecting with your intuition. Pay attention to dreams or subtle synchronicities—they carry guidance now. Emotions may resurface, asking to be released. Honour them without judgement, then let them go. Stillness today isn't wasted—it restores your clarity and prepares you for new beginnings. Trust that by slowing down, you strengthen your inner wisdom.

Affirmation & Gratitude

I honour stillness and reflection, trusting quiet moments to restore peace and clarity.

Taurus
13-July-2026

The Moon enters your sign today, Taurus, bringing renewed vitality and confidence. You may feel motivated to set intentions, begin new projects, or simply show up more authentically. Others notice your calm presence and grounded strength, and opportunities may arise because of it. Don't let self-doubt hold you back—your steady nature already makes you magnetic. Today is about embodying your worth and embracing the power of new beginnings. Trust yourself, and allow your authenticity to shine without hesitation.

Affirmation & Gratitude

I shine with authenticity and confidence, trusting my grounded energy to attract opportunities.

Taurus
14-July-2026

Taurus, resources and self-worth are in focus today. You may feel inclined to organise your finances, review spending, or explore practical ways to create more stability. But the stars also remind you that your true abundance comes from within—your patience, skills, and persistence are powerful assets. Avoid comparing yourself to others; your journey is uniquely yours. A small, consistent step you take today toward security will have long-term benefits. Trust that your steady approach creates solid foundations for prosperity.

Affirmation & Gratitude

I value my worth and trust my steady steps to build lasting prosperity.

Taurus
15-July-2026

Taurus, communication is highlighted today, and your words carry extra weight. You may feel called to write, teach, or share your perspective with others. Conversations could bring clarity, but only if you balance speaking with listening. A short trip or errand may open unexpected doors, offering inspiration from surprising sources. Stay flexible and open-minded—rigid thinking will block insights. Your grounded voice brings calm authority, but remember to let curiosity guide your exchanges. Wisdom comes not only from what you say, but also from what you hear.

Affirmation & Gratitude

I communicate with clarity and openness, trusting dialogue to inspire growth and understanding.

Taurus
16-July-2026

Home and family matters are in focus today, Taurus. You may feel pulled to nurture your living space or resolve domestic issues that have lingered. Emotional conversations could arise, giving you the chance to heal misunderstandings if you stay patient and compassionate. Small actions like tidying, cooking, or refreshing your environment will restore balance. Your home is more than walls —it's a sanctuary that supports your strength. Focus on making it a place of peace, both for yourself and for those you love.

Affirmation & Gratitude

I create harmony in my home, trusting it as the foundation of peace and security.

Taurus
17-July-2026

Taurus, creativity and joy are strongly emphasised today. The stars encourage you to indulge in hobbies, playfulness, and romance. If you've been weighed down by responsibilities, this is your reminder that fun is just as important as work. Express yourself through art, laughter, or affection, and let your inner child lead the way. Romantic energy flows easily, and self-expression will uplift your spirit. Today is about giving yourself permission to enjoy life's beauty, knowing joy is an essential form of healing.

Affirmation & Gratitude

I embrace joy and creativity, trusting play and love to uplift my spirit.

Taurus
18-July-2026

Health, routines, and organisation come into focus today, Taurus. You may feel motivated to refine your schedule, balance your responsibilities, or adopt habits that nurture long-term stability. Don't overwhelm yourself by trying to do everything at once—steady, small steps will carry you furthest. Pay attention to your body's needs, whether that means movement, nourishment, or rest. By aligning productivity with self-care, you strengthen both resilience and peace of mind. The cosmos supports practical adjustments that bring order and balance.

Affirmation & Gratitude

I honour balance in my routines, trusting steady habits to build strength and clarity.

Taurus
19-July-2026

Relationships are highlighted today, Taurus. The cosmos invites you to reflect on balance, fairness, and reciprocity within your connections. Whether in love, friendship, or business, harmony comes from honesty and respect. A heartfelt conversation could help you and someone close realign expectations. If single, this is an excellent day to notice new connections that resonate with your values. Vulnerability is not weakness—it is the pathway to deeper trust. Authenticity is your strongest foundation for building lasting bonds.

Affirmation & Gratitude

I welcome balanced and authentic relationships, trusting openness to deepen my connections.

Taurus
20-July-2026

Deep emotions and transformative energy rise today, Taurus. You may be asked to examine intimacy, shared resources, or lingering fears. Financial matters tied to partnerships may also need attention. While intensity may feel uncomfortable, it carries the gift of renewal. By facing what you've avoided, you create space for growth and empowerment. Release old patterns and step into vulnerability—it will open the door to strength. Transformation is part of your journey, and today reminds you to embrace it with steady courage.

Affirmation & Gratitude

I release old patterns and welcome transformation, trusting renewal to bring strength.

Taurus
21-July-2026

Optimism flows today, Taurus, as the stars encourage you to broaden your horizons. This may come through travel planning, study, or meaningful conversations that shift your perspective. Growth often happens when you say yes to experiences outside your comfort zone. Your earthy nature values stability, but today reminds you that expansion and security can exist together. By blending curiosity with grounded action, you enrich your path and discover new possibilities.

Affirmation & Gratitude

I embrace growth and exploration, trusting curiosity to enrich my journey.

Taurus
22-July-2026

Taurus, career and ambitions are highlighted today as the Sun shifts into Leo. This marks a powerful season for focusing on long-term goals, recognition, and the legacy you're building. You may feel called to take on more responsibility or step into visibility. While this may feel daunting, your grounded persistence is exactly what sets you apart. Today is ideal for strategic planning—align your professional goals with your values and trust that your steady steps will bring lasting rewards. Leadership opportunities may surface now—embrace them with confidence.

Affirmation & Gratitude

I step confidently into my goals, trusting persistence and integrity to shape my legacy.

Taurus
23-July-2026

Taurus, friendships and community connections are emphasised today. You may feel inspired to collaborate with others or share your ideas within a group setting. Conversations with supportive people may spark fresh insights, or a group project may gain momentum. Be mindful of where you invest your energy—align yourself with those who uplift you rather than drain you. This is a day to lean into your social networks, but also to discern which connections truly reflect your values and aspirations.

Affirmation & Gratitude

I attract supportive friendships, trusting collaboration to bring inspiration and joy.

Taurus
24-July-2026

Introspection takes priority today, Taurus. You may feel quieter, preferring to retreat into solitude to recharge. This is an excellent day for meditation, journaling, or processing emotions. The cosmos encourages you to let go of lingering fears or burdens that weigh on you. Dreams or intuitive nudges may carry important guidance, so pay attention to subtle signs. Don't view stillness as wasted time—rest strengthens your clarity and prepares you for the new beginnings that lie ahead.

Affirmation & Gratitude

I honour rest and reflection, trusting solitude to restore my clarity and strength.

Taurus
25-July-2026

The Moon enters your sign today, Taurus, filling you with vitality, confidence, and a sense of renewal. This is an excellent day to set intentions, launch new projects, or show up authentically in your personal and professional life. Others notice your calm steadiness and may be drawn to your presence. Doubts may try to creep in, but your grounded nature is your superpower—trust it fully. Today is about stepping forward with courage and allowing your true self to shine without apology.

Affirmation & Gratitude

I shine with authenticity and confidence, trusting my steady nature to guide new beginnings.

Taurus
26-July-2026

Taurus, today's focus is on resources and self-worth. Financial matters may require attention, or you may feel inspired to create greater stability through practical steps. But this is also about valuing yourself—your skills, determination, and resilience are priceless assets. Avoid comparing yourself to others; your path unfolds in its own time. Small, consistent actions now create long-term prosperity. Trust that by honouring your worth and working steadily, you're building a strong foundation for abundance.

Affirmation & Gratitude

I value my worth and trust my steady steps to create lasting prosperity.

Taurus
27-July-2026

Communication is spotlighted today, Taurus. Conversations may carry extra weight, offering clarity or the chance to resolve misunderstandings. Writing, teaching, or learning is also favoured—your words have influence now. Be mindful of your tone, as it shapes outcomes more than you realise. Unexpected encounters or short trips may spark inspiration. Stay flexible and curious; insights may come from surprising places. By listening as much as you speak, you gain wisdom that helps you move forward with clarity and purpose.

Affirmation & Gratitude

I communicate with clarity and openness, trusting dialogue to inspire growth.

Taurus
28-July-2026

Taurus, your home and family life come into focus. You may feel drawn to nurture your environment, tend to domestic responsibilities, or reconnect with loved ones. Conversations may uncover deeper emotions, but your patience helps restore harmony. Even small actions—like cooking, cleaning, or refreshing a space—can create a sense of renewal. Your home is your sanctuary, and when it feels balanced, it strengthens every part of your life. Today supports grounding yourself through connection with your roots.

Affirmation & Gratitude

I create harmony in my home, trusting it as the foundation of my strength and peace.

Taurus
29-July-2026

Taurus, creativity and joy take centre stage today. The stars encourage you to step into hobbies, romance, and playfulness that refresh your spirit. If life has felt overly serious, today brings a reminder that joy is as important as responsibility. Romantic connections deepen through laughter and shared experiences, while solo pursuits allow your artistic side to flourish. Express yourself without fear of judgement—your creativity is a healing force. By embracing beauty and fun, you recharge and inspire those around you.

Affirmation & Gratitude

I embrace joy and creativity, trusting play and love to restore my spirit.

Taurus
30-July-2026

Taurus, health, habits, and daily routines come into focus. You may feel motivated to get organised, refine schedules, or make adjustments to create balance. Listen to your body—it may be asking for more rest, nourishment, or gentle activity. Avoid overwhelming yourself with unrealistic goals; instead, choose one or two steady changes you can sustain. At work, your methodical approach helps you complete tasks efficiently. By blending productivity with self-care, you build resilience that supports long-term stability.

Affirmation & Gratitude

I honour balance in my routines, trusting small, steady steps to strengthen my well-being.

Taurus
31-July-2026

Relationships take the spotlight today, Taurus. You may feel called to examine how balance and reciprocity play out in your partnerships. A conversation could help resolve tension or deepen trust if approached with honesty and patience. Whether in romance, friendship, or business, authenticity is key. If single, the energy supports meaningful new connections. Don't shy away from vulnerability—it is the foundation of genuine intimacy. Today asks you to show up fully in your connections and allow others to do the same.

Affirmation & Gratitude

I welcome balanced and authentic relationships, trusting honesty to deepen my bonds.

August 2026

Taurus
01-August-2026

Transformation energy rises today, Taurus. Matters of intimacy, shared resources, or emotional depth may come to the surface. While intensity may feel overwhelming, it holds the key to renewal. Old fears or patterns may resurface, giving you the chance to release them for good. Financial agreements may also need review—approach them with clarity and honesty. This is a day to lean into change rather than resist it. Transformation is part of your path, and you're strong enough to embrace it fully.

Affirmation & Gratitude

I release what no longer serves, trusting transformation to bring renewal and strength.

Taurus
02-August-2026

Taurus, optimism and curiosity guide you today. You may feel inspired to explore new ideas, plan travel, or dive into study that expands your perspective. Conversations with people from different backgrounds may spark insights you hadn't considered. Your carthy energy prefers security, but today the stars remind you that growth requires exploration. Balance stability with curiosity, and you'll find yourself enriched by fresh experiences. Today is about stepping outside routine and saying yes to opportunities that broaden your horizon.

Affirmation & Gratitude

I embrace growth and curiosity, trusting new experiences to expand my wisdom.

Taurus
03-August-2026

Taurus, career and ambitions are in the spotlight. Recognition for your steady contributions may come, or you may be asked to step into greater responsibility. This is a good day to assess your professional path and ensure it reflects your values. Success doesn't come overnight—it's built brick by brick, and your persistence is admired. Strategic planning is favoured, and conversations with mentors or authority figures may open doors. Trust that your steady progress is laying the foundation for lasting success.

Affirmation & Gratitude

I move confidently toward my ambitions, trusting persistence to shape my legacy.

Taurus
04-August-2026

Friendships and community ties are highlighted today, Taurus. You may feel inspired to collaborate with others, share ideas, or lean into social connections that uplift you. A group project could gain momentum, or supportive friends may help you see new opportunities. Be discerning, though—notice which connections energise you and which leave you drained. Your loyalty is precious; invest it wisely. Surrounding yourself with people who reflect your values strengthens your dreams and keeps you motivated.

Affirmation & Gratitude

I attract supportive friendships and collaborations that inspire joy and growth.

Taurus
05-August-2026

Taurus, today calls for introspection and rest. You may feel quieter, preferring solitude over social interactions. This is an ideal day for meditation, journaling, or reflecting on what you've achieved recently. Pay attention to dreams or intuitive nudges—they may hold valuable guidance. Old emotions may surface, offering you the chance to release them and lighten your load. Stillness is not wasted time; it's a reset that strengthens your inner clarity. Trust that by pausing now, you're preparing yourself for new beginnings that lie just ahead.

Affirmation & Gratitude

I honour stillness and solitude, trusting reflection to renew my clarity and peace.

Taurus
06-August-2026

The Moon enters your sign today, Taurus, filling you with energy, confidence, and a sense of renewal. You may feel inspired to begin something new or step more fully into your authenticity. Others notice your calm, steady presence, and opportunities may arise simply because you're showing up as yourself. This is a powerful day for setting intentions and embracing personal growth. Trust your instincts and allow your natural magnetism to guide you forward.

Affirmation & Gratitude

I shine with authenticity and confidence, trusting my steady nature to open doors.

Taurus
07-August-2026

Taurus, resources and self-worth are highlighted. You may feel motivated to review your finances, organise budgets, or find ways to strengthen your sense of security. But remember—your greatest wealth is within: your resilience, talents, and determination. Avoid comparing yourself with others; your journey is uniquely yours. A small, practical step taken today could support long-term prosperity. Trust in your ability to create abundance through persistence and patience. The universe is reminding you of the value you carry within.

Affirmation & Gratitude

I value my worth and trust my steady steps to create lasting prosperity.

Taurus
08-August-2026

Communication takes centre stage today, Taurus. You may find yourself engaged in meaningful conversations that bring clarity or inspiration. Writing, teaching, or sharing your ideas may feel natural, and others will value your grounded perspective. Be open-minded new insights may come from surprising sources. Short trips or unexpected encounters could also spark opportunities. Balance speaking with listening, and you'll find wisdom in the exchange. Today is about embracing curiosity and expressing your truth with calm confidence.

Affirmation & Gratitude

I communicate with clarity and openness, trusting dialogue to inspire growth and understanding.

Taurus
09-August-2026

Taurus, home and family take the spotlight today. You may feel drawn to nurture your space, resolve domestic matters, or reconnect with loved ones. Emotional conversations may surface, but your patience and steadiness can guide them toward harmony. Even simple acts—like cooking, tidying, or refreshing your environment—bring peace. Your home is your sanctuary, and when it feels balanced, you feel stronger in every other part of your life. Focus on creating stability and comfort within your private world today.

Affirmation & Gratitude

I create harmony in my home, trusting it as the foundation of my peace and strength.

Taurus
10-August-2026

Creativity, play, and romance are highlighted today, Taurus. The stars encourage you to embrace joy without guilt—your spirit thrives when you give yourself space to enjoy life. Hobbies, artistic expression, or lighthearted connection with others refresh your energy. Romantic encounters may feel especially sweet now, strengthening bonds through laughter and warmth. Don't underestimate the healing power of fun—it's essential for your balance. Today is about celebrating beauty and love, allowing them to uplift and inspire you.

Affirmation & Gratitude

I embrace joy and creativity, trusting play and love to renew my spirit.

Taurus
11-August-2026

Taurus, health and daily routines take focus today. You may feel motivated to refine habits, balance responsibilities, or reorganise your schedule. Listen to your body—it may be asking for care through rest, nourishment, or movement. Approach tasks methodically, but avoid overloading yourself. Consistency, not perfection, brings the best results. By aligning productivity with self-care, you create balance that supports your resilience. The cosmos supports small, practical changes that set you up for long-term well-being.

Affirmation & Gratitude

I honour balance in my routines, trusting steady habits to build strength and stability.

Taurus
12-August-2026

Relationships come into focus today, Taurus. The stars encourage you to reflect on balance, fairness, and authenticity in your partnerships. Whether in romance, friendship, or business, harmony requires mutual respect. You may need to voice your needs honestly, or perhaps listen more deeply to someone close. Vulnerability, though sometimes uncomfortable, can strengthen bonds and deepen trust. If you're single, pay attention to connections that feel genuine—someone new may enter your life with long-term potential. Today is about showing up with openness and patience.

Affirmation & Gratitude

I welcome balance and honesty in my relationships, trusting authenticity to deepen my bonds.

Taurus
13-August-2026

Taurus, emotions run deep today as themes of intimacy, trust, and transformation rise to the surface. Matters involving shared resources or financial commitments may also require your attention. While intensity can feel overwhelming, it's guiding you toward renewal. The stars ask you to face old fears or insecurities with courage—release what no longer serves you and step into growth. Transformation isn't always comfortable, but it always brings strength and clarity. Trust the process; you're creating space for empowerment and healing.

Affirmation & Gratitude

I release old fears and welcome transformation, trusting renewal to bring strength and clarity.

Taurus
14-August-2026

Optimism flows today, Taurus, as the cosmos inspires you to expand your horizons. You may feel called to learn something new, plan travel, or engage in conversations that broaden your perspective. Your earthy nature loves stability, but today asks you to blend it with curiosity and adventure. By opening yourself to new ideas and experiences, you enrich your journey and see your life's bigger picture. Growth comes from courage, and you are strong enough to step outside your comfort zone.

Affirmation & Gratitude

I embrace new horizons with courage, trusting curiosity to enrich my journey.

Taurus
15-August-2026

Career and ambitions take the spotlight today, Taurus. Recognition for your consistent efforts may come, or a responsibility may be placed in your hands. While this could feel like pressure, it's also an opportunity to show your strength and reliability. Today favours long-term planning—think about where you want to be in the coming years and set practical steps to get there. Trust that persistence is your superpower; it's building the legacy you're meant to create.

Affirmation & Gratitude

I step steadily toward my ambitions, trusting patience and persistence to shape my future.

Taurus
16-August-2026

Taurus, friendships and community ties are emphasised today. You may feel inspired to collaborate, share ideas, or connect with supportive people who share your values. Group projects gain momentum now, and conversations may spark exciting insights. At the same time, you may recognise which connections no longer feel aligned. Invest your loyalty in those who uplift and energise you. Remember, surrounding yourself with positive influences amplifies your strength and gives your dreams a powerful boost.

Affirmation & Gratitude

I attract supportive friendships and collaborations, trusting community to inspire my growth.

Taurus
17-August-2026

Today invites reflection and solitude, Taurus. You may feel less social, preferring quiet moments to recharge. Use this time for journaling, meditation, or simply slowing down enough to hear your inner voice. Your intuition is heightened, and dreams or subtle signs may carry messages worth noting. Release old worries that have been weighing you down—this is your chance to reset. Rest is not weakness; it is fuel for the soul. Honour your need for quiet and you'll emerge stronger.

Affirmation & Gratitude

I honour stillness and reflection, trusting solitude to restore my peace and clarity.

Taurus
18-August-2026

The Moon moves into your sign today, Taurus, infusing you with renewed energy, confidence, and vitality. You may feel ready to start fresh projects, make bold choices, or express yourself more authentically. Others notice your calm authority and may be drawn to your grounded energy. This is a powerful time for setting personal intentions and embracing your worth. Don't doubt yourself—your authenticity is your greatest strength, and today reminds you to step fully into it.

Affirmation & Gratitude

I shine with confidence and authenticity, trusting my steady nature to guide new beginnings.

Taurus
19-August-2026

Taurus, resources and finances are spotlighted today. You may feel motivated to review budgets, manage possessions, or consider ways to build long-term security. This isn't just about money—it's also about valuing your skills and inner strengths. Recognise how much you already contribute, even if you sometimes underestimate yourself. Avoid comparing your path with others; your steady pace creates sustainable results. A practical step you take today could have lasting rewards. The universe is reminding you to anchor yourself in self-worth and confidence.

Affirmation & Gratitude

I value my worth and trust my steady steps to create lasting abundance.

Taurus
20-August-2026

Communication flows strongly today, Taurus. Meaningful conversations could bring clarity, inspiration, or even healing. You may find yourself writing, teaching, or sharing your ideas in ways that resonate with others. Listen as much as you speak—insight comes through both giving and receiving. Be flexible in your thinking; new perspectives may shift your approach. Short trips or unexpected interactions could also spark fresh opportunities. Trust that your grounded voice carries weight and wisdom when expressed with authenticity.

Affirmation & Gratitude

I communicate with clarity and openness, trusting dialogue to bring insight and connection.

Taurus
21-August-2026

Taurus, your home and family life are emphasised today. You may feel called to nurture your living space, address domestic matters, or reconnect with loved ones. Emotional conversations may reveal truths that bring deeper understanding, provided you approach them with patience. Even small tasks like tidying or refreshing your space restore balance and peace. Your home is your sanctuary, and creating harmony there supports you in all other areas of life. Focus on strengthening your roots and cultivating comfort.

Affirmation & Gratitude

I create harmony in my home, trusting it as the foundation of my peace and strength.

Taurus
22-August-2026

Creativity, play, and romance are highlighted today, Taurus. The cosmos invites you to enjoy life more fully, whether through hobbies, laughter, or affection. Joy isn't frivolous—it's nourishment for your spirit. Romance may blossom, or existing bonds may feel lighter and more connected. Creative energy flows strongly, so allow yourself to explore beauty and fun without self-criticism. Today is a reminder that happiness and productivity are not opposites—they feed each other when balanced. Let your heart lead the way.

Affirmation & Gratitude

I embrace joy and creativity, trusting play and love to uplift my spirit.

Taurus
23-August-2026

Taurus, health and daily routines are in focus. The Sun shifts into Virgo today, further emphasising balance, organisation, and practical adjustments. You may feel called to refine habits, reorganise your schedule, or take steps toward greater wellness. Don't overwhelm yourself with drastic changes—your strength lies in persistence and steady improvement. Today is about creating order that supports your long-term peace of mind. Trust your ability to ground yourself in routines that nourish both body and spirit.

Affirmation & Gratitude

I honour balance in my routines, trusting small, steady steps to build strength and stability.

Taurus
24-August-2026

Relationships are highlighted today, Taurus. The stars encourage you to reflect on balance, reciprocity, and honesty within your partnerships. You may feel called to clarify expectations or have an important conversation with someone close. Vulnerability may feel uncomfortable but leads to deeper trust. If you're single, this is an excellent day for noticing connections that align with your values. Remember, true harmony is not about avoiding conflict—it's about resolving it with respect and openness.

Affirmation & Gratitude

I welcome balanced and authentic relationships, trusting honesty to strengthen my bonds.

Taurus
25-August-2026

Transformation energy surrounds you, Taurus. Emotional intensity may rise, highlighting matters of trust, intimacy, or shared resources. Financial agreements could require review, or you may feel prompted to face insecurities you've carried quietly. While this process can feel confronting, it is also liberating. The cosmos is asking you to release what no longer serves your growth. By leaning into vulnerability, you discover empowerment and resilience. Trust the process of change—it clears space for renewal and clarity.

Affirmation & Gratitude

I release old fears and welcome transformation, trusting renewal to bring strength and peace.

Taurus
26-August-2026

Taurus, optimism flows today as the stars encourage you to expand your perspective. You may feel drawn to learning, exploring, or opening your mind through meaningful conversations. Travel planning or study may also be highlighted. While your earthy nature seeks stability, growth often requires stepping beyond the familiar. A fresh perspective could shift how you see your current situation, giving you renewed hope. This is a day to embrace curiosity and say yes to experiences that stretch your worldview. Adventure and security can co-exist when balanced with intention.

Affirmation & Gratitude

I welcome new horizons, trusting curiosity and exploration to enrich my journey.

Taurus
27-August-2026

Taurus, your career and ambitions take the spotlight. Recognition for your steady efforts may arrive, or you could be asked to step into leadership. While added responsibility can feel daunting, trust your persistence—it has prepared you for this. Today is also excellent for long-term planning. Map out your goals and ensure they reflect your true values. Avoid chasing quick wins; focus instead on the legacy you want to build. Your reliability is your greatest asset, and others notice your grounded authority.

Affirmation & Gratitude

I step forward with confidence, trusting persistence and integrity to shape my success.

Taurus
28-August-2026

Friendships and community connections are highlighted today, Taurus. You may feel uplifted by spending time with supportive people who share your vision. A group project could gain momentum, or you may gain encouragement from your social networks. At the same time, you may become aware of connections that no longer align with your energy. Invest your loyalty where it is reciprocated and valued. Today is about recognising the strength of collaboration and surrounding yourself with people who celebrate your growth.

Affirmation & Gratitude

I attract supportive friendships and collaborations, trusting community to inspire and uplift me.

Taurus
29-August-2026

Taurus, today invites introspection and solitude. You may feel less social, preferring to withdraw into quiet spaces that allow reflection. Dreams or intuitive nudges could bring guidance, so pay attention to the subtle. Old emotions may rise, asking to be acknowledged and released. This is a perfect day for journaling, meditation, or simply slowing down. Don't mistake rest for stagnation—this is the pause that renews your strength. Trust that stillness creates clarity, preparing you for the fresh beginnings soon to come.

Affirmation & Gratitude

I honour stillness and solitude, trusting quiet moments to restore peace and clarity.

Taurus
30-August-2026

The Moon moves into your sign today, Taurus, filling you with vitality, confidence, and a sense of renewal. You may feel inspired to set intentions, pursue a new goal, or embrace your authenticity more fully. Others notice your grounded strength, and your presence alone can draw opportunities your way. Trust your instincts and don't downplay your talents. This is a day to embody your worth and claim space unapologetically. Fresh energy surrounds you—use it to step boldly toward what matters most.

Affirmation & Gratitude

I shine with confidence and authenticity, trusting my steady strength to guide new beginnings.

Taurus
31-August-2026

Taurus, your focus shifts to resources and self-worth today. Financial matters may require attention, or you may feel motivated to strengthen your sense of stability through practical steps. Beyond money, the stars remind you to value your inner wealth—your patience, resilience, and dedication are priceless. Avoid comparing yourself to others; your journey is uniquely yours. A grounded choice you make today could support prosperity in the long term. Trust that small steps now create lasting abundance.

Affirmation & Gratitude

I value my worth and trust my steady actions to build long-term prosperity.

September 2026

Taurus
01-September-2026

Taurus, the year begins with a gentle but steady cosmic push urging you to release outdated expectations and embrace a refreshed mindset. Venus, your ruler, is stirring connections in both love and finance, making today an ideal moment to align your values with your long-term goals. Don't let the small distractions of others' dramas throw you off balance. Instead, ground yourself in practical steps—tidy a space, make a list, or plan your week. This isn't about rushing forward but about setting a steady pace that feels true to you.

Affirmation & Gratitude

I welcome this new year with steady grace, trusting my values and planting seeds of lasting abundance.

Taurus
02-September-2026

Taurus, the year begins with a gentle but steady cosmic push urging you to release outdated expectations and embrace a refreshed mindset. Venus, your ruler, is stirring connections in both love and finance, making today an ideal moment to align your values with your long-term goals. Don't let the small distractions of others' dramas throw you off balance. Instead, ground yourself in practical steps—tidy a space, make a list, or plan your week. This isn't about rushing forward but about setting a steady pace that feels true to you.

Affirmation & Gratitude

I welcome this new year with steady grace, trusting my values and planting seeds of lasting abundance.

Taurus
03-September-2026

Today brings you a deeper sense of clarity, Taurus, especially around relationships. You may notice which bonds are uplifting and which drain your energy. The Moon highlights communication, encouraging you to speak truthfully, but also listen with patience. It's not about winning debates—it's about creating balance. A small conversation may lead to surprising understanding if you remain calm and open. Don't dismiss intuitive nudges; your inner voice is whispering the right path forward. Ground yourself in routine, but leave room for meaningful interactions that nurture your soul.

Affirmation & Gratitude

I honour the connections that bring peace and release those that no longer align with my heart's truth.

Taurus
04-September-2026

Taurus, today the stars spotlight your finances and personal worth. A sudden opportunity to improve your income may appear, but it requires you to step outside your usual comfort zone. Don't let fear of change keep you from progress. Remember, security isn't just about money—it's about self-trust and knowing your skills have value. Spend time reflecting on how you can make your talents more visible. The key is believing in your own power. The universe is aligning to reward steady, practical action taken now.

Affirmation & Gratitude

I believe in my skills, trusting that my work and talents attract prosperity and recognition.

Taurus
05-September-2026

You may feel torn between rest and productivity today, Taurus. The Moon encourages downtime, but Mars is pulling you toward action. Balance is your gift—find a rhythm that allows both. Perhaps tackle one key task, then give yourself permission to relax without guilt. Don't underestimate the power of quiet reflection; insights often come when you're still. A new perspective may arrive through a dream, meditation, or even a peaceful walk. Allow yourself to enjoy the softer pace of the day without feeling you must prove yourself.

Affirmation & Gratitude

I balance rest and action, trusting that both serve my highest growth and bring me strength.

Taurus
06-September-2026

Taurus, today is perfect for clearing away clutter—both physical and emotional. You've been holding onto more than you need, and the stars urge you to let go. What feels heavy or outdated no longer belongs in your space. A release today will invite fresh opportunities tomorrow. Relationships may also benefit from honest conversations about boundaries and needs. Don't be afraid to express your feelings; you'll be surprised at how freeing it is. Transformation doesn't always come in loud ways—sometimes it's the quiet act of letting go.

Affirmation & Gratitude

I release what no longer serves me and invite fresh energy, clarity, and freedom into my life.

Taurus
07-September-2026

The energy shifts today, Taurus, pushing you toward expansion. This may show up as learning, travel planning, or simply seeing life from a wider lens. Your practical nature prefers stability, but sometimes adventure calls. Say yes to something new—even if it's small, like reading a book outside your usual interests or trying a different route. The universe is inviting you to broaden your perspective. Growth doesn't require abandoning security; it means blending curiosity with grounded action. The stars are nudging you to trust the unknown with steady faith.

Affirmation & Gratitude

I embrace new experiences, knowing they expand my heart, mind, and spirit while keeping me grounded.

Taurus
08-September-2026

Taurus, today highlights partnerships. Whether in romance, friendship, or business, you're asked to look at how balance plays out. Are you giving more than you're receiving, or holding back when you should be more open? The stars encourage collaboration, but also healthy boundaries. A moment of honesty could strengthen trust, even if it feels uncomfortable at first. Don't be afraid to show vulnerability—it doesn't weaken you, it deepens your connections. Remember, harmony in relationships comes from authenticity, not perfection.

Affirmation & Gratitude

I allow honest connections to thrive, creating relationships built on mutual respect, balance, and truth.

Taurus
09-September-2026

Taurus, today your focus shifts to health, daily routines, and the way you take care of your body and mind. The cosmos encourages small but steady adjustments that will support you long-term. Perhaps it's preparing nourishing meals, moving your body with intention, or simply reorganising your schedule to ease unnecessary stress. Don't underestimate the ripple effect of minor changes—what feels like a small step today can become a strong foundation for your future. Pay attention to what your body tells you; it's speaking clearly now. Honour it, and you'll notice renewed strength.

Affirmation & Gratitude

I nurture myself with care and honour my body's wisdom, knowing each small step builds lasting well-being.

Taurus
10-September-2026

Your creative spark is ignited today, Taurus, as planetary alignments stir your imagination and encourage self-expression. This isn't about perfection or impressing others—it's about playing with ideas, colour, words, or music simply for the joy of it. You may feel drawn to hobbies, art, or even spontaneous adventures that remind you of your inner child. Romance is also favoured, with a playful tone infusing conversations and connections. If you've felt weighed down lately, today offers a chance to lighten your heart and rediscover joy in simple pleasures. Creativity is your healing medicine now.

Affirmation & Gratitude

I embrace creativity and joy, allowing playfulness and passion to guide my heart toward freedom and delight.

Taurus
11-September-2026

Taurus, your attention turns toward work and responsibility today. While you're not afraid of hard effort, the stars caution you to avoid pushing yourself beyond your natural rhythm. Instead, focus on smart organisation and prioritising what really matters. If you've been chasing too many tasks at once, streamline. Conversations with authority figures may surface—be clear, calm, and grounded in your values. Recognition is possible now, but it will come through consistent effort rather than flashy gestures. Remember, your strength is persistence and reliability. Trust that showing up steadily will open doors for you.

Affirmation & Gratitude

I move steadily forward, trusting persistence and organisation to bring me the success and recognition I deserve.

Taurus
12-September-2026

Today the Moon shines on your friendships, networks, and community ties. Taurus, you may feel called to connect with like-minded people or revisit goals you've set with others. Collaboration is highlighted, but so is the importance of knowing who truly has your back. Not every connection is meant to last forever, and you may sense shifts in your social circle. Follow your instincts—gravitate toward those who inspire, uplift, and encourage growth. Whether it's sharing a dream or lending support, your presence is valuable. The right people see your worth without you needing to prove it.

Affirmation & Gratitude

I attract supportive connections that celebrate who I am and encourage my growth and dreams.

Taurus
13-September-2026

A deeply introspective energy surrounds you today, Taurus. You may feel quieter, more contemplative, and drawn to your inner world. Use this time to reflect on recent choices and how they've shaped your current path. The cosmos is encouraging release—old fears, grudges, or doubts can be acknowledged and gently put to rest. Dreams may hold special messages; pay attention to what stirs beneath the surface. Though you may feel less social, this is a healing pause, not a setback. By allowing yourself this depth, you create space for renewal and clarity moving forward.

Affirmation & Gratitude

I honour stillness and reflection, trusting that my inner wisdom guides me toward peace and renewal.

Taurus
14-September-2026

Taurus, today you step into renewed confidence and self-assurance as the stars light up your first house of identity. You may feel a boost of energy that encourages you to take bold steps forward, whether in your appearance, personal goals, or simply the way you carry yourself. The world notices your steady presence, and opportunities may come your way because you've allowed yourself to be visible. This is a reminder that you don't need to force change—authenticity itself shines brightly. Trust your worth and let your grounded nature be your greatest strength.

Affirmation & Gratitude

I shine with authenticity, allowing my true self to be seen, valued, and celebrated.

Taurus
15-September-2026

Today highlights your resources, Taurus, both financial and personal. You may find yourself reviewing budgets, expenses, or ways to strengthen security. But the stars also remind you that true abundance isn't measured only in money—it's also your skills, talents, and connections. A conversation around shared resources or investments could arise; approach it with practicality and calm. You're building something stable for the future, and patience will reward you. Resist the urge to compare your path to others—you're on your own timeline. Steadiness is your gift, and today it pays off.

Affirmation & Gratitude

I value my resources and trust in my ability to create lasting security and abundance.

Taurus
16-September-2026

Taurus, today brings focus to communication, learning, and the way you share your thoughts with others. A conversation may spark a new idea, or you could find yourself drawn to writing, studying, or simply soaking up knowledge. Your natural practicality allows you to turn inspiration into something tangible, so don't dismiss even the smallest insight. Be mindful of your words, though—once spoken, they carry weight. Choose clarity and kindness over impatience. If you've been considering a short trip, planning now will benefit you later. The universe is opening channels for mental expansion.

Affirmation & Gratitude

I communicate with clarity, absorbing wisdom and sharing my words with honesty, kindness, and purpose.

Taurus
17-September-2026

The stars shine a light on your home and family life today, Taurus. Domestic matters may need your attention, whether that means household tasks, family conversations, or simply carving out time to rest in your sacred space. If emotions run high, stay grounded and approach matters with calm patience—your steadiness helps restore balance. A memory from the past may resurface, offering insight into how far you've come. Whether you're reorganising a room, cooking for loved ones, or sitting quietly, nurture the space that nurtures you. Stability at home becomes your anchor for growth outside.

Affirmation & Gratitude

I create peace and stability within my home, honouring it as the foundation for my strength and happiness.

Taurus
18-September-2026

Taurus, romance and creativity sparkle today. Whether partnered or single, your heart is ready to feel more joy, warmth, and expression. If you've been holding back, let your playful side emerge—sing, dance, paint, or simply laugh without restraint. A relationship could deepen through shared joy or lighthearted connection. This is not a day for heavy responsibility; instead, it invites fun, affection, and self-expression. Trust that when you follow your heart, others are drawn to your authentic glow. Your creativity is not frivolous—it's essential to keeping your spirit alive and thriving.

Affirmation & Gratitude

I embrace joy, love, and creativity, allowing my playful spirit to shine and uplift those around me.

Taurus
19-September-2026

Today asks you to focus on your health and daily balance. Taurus, it's time to tune into your body's rhythm and see where adjustments are needed. Are you resting enough? Drinking water? Honouring your body with movement? Even small shifts—stretching, walking, or eating mindfully—make a difference now. Work tasks may demand attention too, but don't let stress build unchecked. Creating a routine that blends productivity and well-being is your path forward. Remember, your body is the vessel through which all your dreams flow, and nurturing it is an investment in your future.

Affirmation & Gratitude

I respect my body's needs and create balance in my daily life, honouring health as my true wealth.

Taurus
20-September-2026

Taurus, the cosmos highlights relationships again, asking you to look at balance and reciprocity. A partner, friend, or colleague may seek your support, but check in with yourself first—are you giving too much? Or are you holding back from being fully open? The truth lies in honest connection, not overextending or withholding. Today encourages you to see partnerships as mirrors; what you notice in others may reflect something within you. By approaching conversations with kindness and courage, you strengthen trust. Relationships that are aligned will grow stronger under today's energy.

Affirmation & Gratitude

I welcome balanced, loving connections that reflect my truth and honour mutual respect and care.

Taurus
21-September-2026

Today may stir deeper emotions, Taurus, as the Moon highlights themes of intimacy, vulnerability, and shared resources. You may be asked to trust someone with your heart, money, or secrets, and though it feels exposing, leaning into trust can bring growth. If fears arise, face them gently—acknowledge, then release. Transformation is the gift here, but it requires letting go of control and embracing depth. This is also a good day for reviewing finances or agreements with honesty. Healing comes when you allow yourself to be seen fully, without hiding.

Affirmation & Gratitude

I trust the process of transformation and allow vulnerability to deepen love, healing, and understanding.

Taurus
22-September-2026

Taurus, a wave of optimism lifts you today as the stars encourage expansion, learning, and seeing life from a bigger perspective. This could mean planning future travels, signing up for a course, or simply opening your mind to fresh philosophies. Opportunities come when you're willing to step outside of the comfortable and consider what else is possible. Your earthy nature prefers security, but growth often means taking measured risks. Say yes to something inspiring today—it could shape the direction of your year. Your soul is asking for adventure.

Affirmation & Gratitude

I embrace new horizons with courage, trusting each experience expands my wisdom and joy.

Taurus
23-September-2026

Taurus, today's cosmic energy shines on your ambitions and long-term goals. You may feel inspired to take bold steps toward career advancement or finally map out the path you want for the year ahead. Recognition is possible if you've been consistent, but don't expect overnight results. Your earthy patience is your superpower, and others admire the stability you bring. Conversations with mentors or authority figures may surface—approach them with confidence and clarity. Trust that your reliability and dedication are being noticed. The seeds you plant today have the potential to flourish into lasting success.

Affirmation & Gratitude

I take steady steps toward my ambitions, knowing patience and persistence bring lasting success and recognition.

Taurus
24-September-2026

Today invites you to connect with friends, groups, or networks, Taurus. Collaborative energy is strong, and you may feel inspired by conversations with like-minded souls. Whether it's brainstorming with colleagues, reconnecting with old friends, or sharing ideas with your community, the exchange of energy lifts your spirit. Stay open to invitations, even if they're outside your comfort zone—you may meet someone who sparks inspiration or offers unexpected support. This is also a good day to set intentions for your role in a team. You don't have to do everything alone; unity strengthens you.

Affirmation & Gratitude

I welcome connections that inspire growth, collaboration, and joy, knowing I thrive when I share my journey with others.

Taurus
25-September-2026

Taurus, the stars guide you inward today. You may feel quieter, more reflective, and drawn to moments of solitude. Rather than resisting, embrace this as a chance to reset your spirit. Your dreams or intuition may bring guidance, so pay attention to symbols, nudges, or synchronicities. This is a day for rest, gentle self-care, and releasing worries you've carried too long. By allowing yourself to pause, you prepare for the fresh energy that's coming. Trust that not every day requires action—sometimes the most powerful progress is made in stillness and silence.

Affirmation & Gratitude

I honour rest and reflection, trusting that stillness restores my clarity and strengthens my spirit.

Taurus
26-September-2026

Energy lifts today, Taurus, as the Moon moves into your sign, spotlighting your confidence, appearance, and personal goals. You may feel a burst of vitality and a renewed sense of direction. This is the perfect time to start something new or make your presence known. Others notice your steady strength and grounded nature, and opportunities may appear simply because you're showing up authentically. If doubts creep in, remember that you don't need to rush; your steady pace is enough. Today is about embodying your worth and embracing the power of being yourself fully.

Affirmation & Gratitude

I shine with confidence, embracing my true self and stepping forward with strength and authenticity.

Taurus
27-September-2026

Taurus, today encourages a deeper look at your resources—both financial and emotional. You may feel motivated to organise budgets, review investments, or strengthen security. But the universe also reminds you that wealth isn't just money—it's the skills, resilience, and connections you carry. Someone may offer advice or propose a financial discussion, so be ready to approach with calm practicality. Don't let comparison undermine your confidence; your journey is unique. By honouring your values, you'll attract prosperity that feels aligned and lasting. Today is about trusting your ability to create abundance in your way.

Affirmation & Gratitude

I value my unique path and trust my ability to create lasting prosperity rooted in my true values.

Taurus
28-September-2026

Communication is highlighted today, Taurus. The stars encourage you to share your ideas openly, whether through a conversation, writing, or teaching. Your words carry weight and can bring clarity to others, but remember to listen as much as you speak. Someone may reveal information that helps you see things differently. Short trips or changes to your daily routine could bring new perspectives. Stay curious and open, even if it means stepping beyond your usual comfort zone. Inspiration flows when you embrace fresh viewpoints and trust the exchange of ideas.

Affirmation & Gratitude

I communicate with openness and curiosity, trusting my words and listening bring insight and connection.

Taurus
29-September-2026

Home and family matters come into focus today, Taurus. You may feel called to nurture your space or spend time reconnecting with loved ones. Domestic projects, from cooking a meal to rearranging furniture, can bring surprising comfort and grounding. If tensions arise in family conversations, use your calm patience to guide the atmosphere back to balance. Your home is not just a structure—it's the foundation of your energy. By tending to it, you create a sanctuary that sustains you. Focus on building warmth and security in your personal world today.

Affirmation & Gratitude

I create harmony in my home, knowing it supports my peace, stability, and growth.

Taurus
30-September-2026

Taurus, today your creativity and joy are highlighted. You may feel drawn to hobbies, art, or simply having fun for fun's sake. Romance also glimmers under today's skies, with opportunities to express affection more openly. If life has felt heavy, today is your chance to lighten the load and reconnect with laughter. Don't underestimate the healing power of play; it balances the serious responsibilities you often carry. Give yourself permission to indulge in simple pleasures—a walk, a song, or a heartfelt chat. Your soul thrives when it is allowed to shine with joy.

Affirmation & Gratitude

I embrace joy and creativity, allowing playfulness and love to uplift and heal my spirit.

October 2026

Taurus
01-October-2026

Taurus, your resources and self-worth take the spotlight. You may feel motivated to review finances, set new savings goals, or explore opportunities for long-term security. Beyond money, this is also about recognising your inner value—your patience, loyalty, and skills are assets in themselves. Avoid comparison with others; your path unfolds in its own divine timing. Practical decisions made today could carry long-term rewards. By valuing yourself, you naturally attract abundance in all forms.

Affirmation & Gratitude

I value my worth and trust my steady steps to create lasting prosperity.

Taurus
02-October-2026

Communication is favoured today, Taurus. Important conversations may bring clarity or resolve lingering issues. Writing, teaching, or sharing ideas flows smoothly, and your grounded perspective resonates with others. Be mindful of your words, as they carry influence. Listen carefully too—wisdom may come from unexpected sources. Short trips or chance encounters could spark new opportunities or insights. Flexibility in thought is key. The cosmos encourages you to blend curiosity with practicality to gain the most benefit today.

Affirmation & Gratitude

I communicate with clarity and openness, trusting dialogue to inspire growth and understanding.

Taurus
03-October-2026

Taurus, home and family matters are highlighted. You may feel called to nurture your environment, refresh your space, or connect with loved ones more deeply. Emotions may run higher today, but your patience and calm presence can help smooth over tensions. Even small gestures, like cooking a meal or rearranging a room, bring comfort and renewal. Your home is not only where you live—it reflects your inner state. By cultivating harmony here, you create peace that ripples into every part of life.

Affirmation & Gratitude

I create peace and harmony in my home, trusting it as the foundation of my strength.

Taurus
04-October-2026

Creativity, joy, and romance are emphasised today. Taurus, this is a day to let your spirit feel lighter and playful. Whether through art, laughter, hobbies, or affection, your heart is ready to express itself. Joy isn't a distraction—it's fuel for your soul. Romantic connections are strengthened through shared happiness, while solo pursuits remind you of your natural creativity. Let yourself enjoy beauty without guilt; your grounded energy is lifted when balanced with fun and self-expression.

Affirmation & Gratitude

I embrace joy and creativity, trusting play and love to nourish my spirit.

Taurus
05-October-2026

Taurus, health and routines are in focus today. You may feel inspired to get organised, refine habits, or create a more balanced schedule. Your body may also call for attention—listen and respond with care, whether through nourishment, rest, or gentle movement. Productivity flows best when balanced with self-care. Don't pressure yourself to achieve everything at once; steady progress creates lasting results. Today supports practical steps that strengthen your resilience and bring clarity to your daily rhythm.

Affirmation & Gratitude

I honour balance in my routines, trusting steady steps to strengthen my well-being.

Taurus
06-October-2026

Relationships are highlighted today, Taurus. The cosmos encourages you to reflect on balance and reciprocity in your connections. You may feel called to clarify expectations or have a meaningful conversation with someone close. Harmony isn't about perfection; it's about authenticity and mutual respect. Vulnerability may be required, but it also deepens trust. If single, new encounters may feel promising. Today is about investing in the partnerships that nurture you while ensuring your needs are met too.

Affirmation & Gratitude

I welcome authentic and balanced relationships, trusting honesty to deepen my bonds.

Taurus
07-October-2026

Taurus, today brings transformative energy as intimacy, trust, and shared resources move into focus. You may be called to face fears or insecurities that you've kept hidden. While this can feel uncomfortable, leaning into honesty allows growth and renewal. Financial matters connected to others may also require review—clarity is key here. Transformation clears away what no longer serves, opening the path to empowerment. Trust that letting go is not a loss but a step toward greater strength and freedom.

Affirmation & Gratitude

I release what no longer serves me, trusting transformation to bring strength and clarity.

Taurus
08-October-2026

Optimism and expansion guide you today, Taurus. You may feel inspired to study, plan travel, or explore new philosophies that shift your worldview. Conversations with people from different walks of life could spark meaningful insights. Your earthy nature values stability, but today encourages you to blend it with curiosity. Growth doesn't require abandoning security—it simply means allowing yourself to stretch beyond the familiar. Say yes to opportunities that broaden your perspective. Today, curiosity is your most powerful tool.

Affirmation & Gratitude

I embrace curiosity and growth, trusting new experiences to expand my wisdom.

Taurus
09-October-2026

Career and long-term ambitions take the spotlight today. Taurus, recognition for your efforts may arrive, or you could be asked to step into leadership. While pressure may feel heavy, remember that persistence and reliability are your greatest strengths. Use this energy to reassess your goals—are they aligned with your values and dreams? Practical planning now will carry you further than rushing ahead. Trust that your slow and steady pace is building something strong and lasting.

Affirmation & Gratitude

I step steadily toward my goals, trusting persistence and patience to shape my success.

Taurus
10-October-2026

Friendships and community ties are highlighted, Taurus. A group project may gather momentum, or you may find joy in connecting with supportive people who share your vision. The energy is collaborative and inspiring, helping you see possibilities you might not have noticed alone. At the same time, you may need to step back from connections that no longer align with your values. Today is about surrounding yourself with people who celebrate your growth and uplift your spirit.

Affirmation & Gratitude

I attract supportive friendships, trusting collaboration to inspire and strengthen me.

Taurus
11-October-2026

Taurus, today invites introspection and rest. You may feel a need for solitude to process emotions or recharge your energy. Dreams, meditation, or journaling could bring valuable insights now, so pay attention to subtle signs and inner whispers. Old patterns may resurface, offering you the chance to release them once and for all. This is not a day for rushing ahead but for stillness and reflection. Trust that rest is a form of progress, restoring clarity for what's next.

Affirmation & Gratitude

I honour rest and reflection, trusting stillness to restore my clarity and peace.

Taurus
12-October-2026

The Moon enters your sign, Taurus, infusing you with confidence, vitality, and a sense of renewal. You may feel ready to set intentions, begin a new project, or simply express yourself more authentically. Others are drawn to your calm strength, and opportunities may come because you're shining as your true self. Today is about embracing your worth and stepping boldly into fresh energy. Don't underestimate how magnetic you are when you show up fully and unapologetically.

Affirmation & Gratitude

I shine with authenticity and confidence, trusting my steady nature to open new paths.

Taurus
13-October-2026

Taurus, your focus turns to finances, possessions, and self-worth. You may feel prompted to organise budgets, review your spending, or consider ways to build greater stability. But remember—true abundance is not only material. Your patience, skills, and resilience are also forms of wealth. Avoid comparing yourself with others; your steady approach builds sustainable prosperity. A grounded decision made today could support your security in the long term. Honour both your practical and inner resources.

Affirmation & Gratitude

I value my worth and trust my steady steps to create lasting abundance.

Taurus
14-October-2026

Taurus, communication is spotlighted today. Conversations may hold extra weight, offering opportunities for clarity, healing, or inspiration. Writing, teaching, or sharing your thoughts flows naturally, and your steady perspective resonates with others. Be mindful of tone, as your words carry influence. Stay open-minded—wisdom may come from unexpected places. A short trip or spontaneous meeting could also open doors. This is a day to balance speaking with listening, ensuring dialogue becomes a two-way exchange that enriches everyone involved.

Affirmation & Gratitude

I communicate with clarity and openness, trusting dialogue to bring insight and growth.

Taurus
15-October-2026

Taurus, your home and family life are highlighted. You may feel pulled to nurture your space, resolve domestic matters, or connect more deeply with loved ones. Emotions may run higher than usual, but your patience can help restore harmony. Even simple actions like tidying, cooking, or refreshing your environment create grounding. Your home reflects your inner state, and by bringing peace here, you strengthen all other areas of your life. Today is about cultivating a safe and supportive foundation.

Affirmation & Gratitude

I create peace and harmony in my home, trusting it as the foundation of my strength.

Taurus
16-October-2026

Joy, creativity, and romance shine brightly today. Taurus, the stars encourage you to let go of seriousness and reconnect with your playful side. Engage in hobbies, art, or music, or spend time laughing with loved ones. Romance is favoured, as lighthearted energy fosters deeper bonds. Fun is not a distraction—it is a vital form of nourishment. By expressing yourself freely, you replenish your spirit and remind yourself that beauty and love are part of your strength.

Affirmation & Gratitude

I embrace joy and creativity, trusting play and love to uplift and renew my spirit.

Taurus
17-October-2026

Taurus, health and routines are emphasised today. You may feel motivated to refine habits, improve organisation, or create balance between work and rest. Your body may signal what it needs—whether that's more sleep, better nourishment, or physical activity. Productivity flows smoothly when paired with self-care. Avoid overwhelming yourself with perfectionism; steady progress is what matters. This is a day to anchor yourself in simple, sustainable practices that support long-term well-being and resilience.

Affirmation & Gratitude

I honour balance in my routines, trusting steady habits to strengthen my well-being.

Taurus
18-October-2026

Relationships come into focus today, Taurus. Whether in love, friendship, or business, harmony depends on honesty and respect. A heart-to-heart conversation may bring clarity or help you set healthier boundaries. If single, new encounters could carry meaningful potential. Vulnerability deepens trust, so don't shy away from showing your true self. Balance is key—make sure your needs are honoured alongside others'. Authenticity is what keeps relationships strong, and today is about investing in bonds that uplift you.

Affirmation & Gratitude

I welcome balanced and authentic relationships, trusting honesty to deepen my connections.

Taurus
19-October-2026

Taurus, transformation energy surrounds you as issues of intimacy, shared resources, and personal growth rise to the surface. You may feel prompted to release fears, outdated habits, or unhealthy attachments. Financial agreements may also need review—take a practical but honest approach. Though the process may feel intense, it opens the path to empowerment. By facing what you've avoided, you reclaim your strength. Today is about honouring vulnerability as the gateway to healing and resilience.

Affirmation & Gratitude

I release what no longer serves, trusting transformation to bring renewal and empowerment.

Taurus
20-October-2026

Expansion and optimism fill your day, Taurus. You may feel drawn to explore new ideas, study, or connect with people who broaden your perspective. Planning travel or future opportunities is also favoured. Your earthy energy often craves stability, but today asks you to step outside your comfort zone. Growth doesn't mean abandoning security; it means blending it with exploration. Be willing to say yes to new experiences—you'll find wisdom and inspiration along the way.

Affirmation & Gratitude

I embrace curiosity and growth, trusting new experiences to enrich my journey.

Taurus
21-October-2026

Taurus, career and long-term ambitions are in the spotlight today. Recognition for your persistence may arrive, or you could be asked to step into a leadership role. While this may bring added pressure, trust that you've been preparing for this moment. Today is ideal for planning—look at your goals and ensure they align with your values. Success isn't about rushing ahead but about building something sustainable. Your calm steadiness inspires others, and opportunities may arise because of your reliability.

Affirmation & Gratitude

I step steadily toward my goals, trusting persistence and patience to shape lasting success.

Taurus
22-October-2026

Friendships and community energy are emphasised, Taurus. Collaboration brings inspiration, and group projects may move forward with ease. Conversations with supportive people may spark new opportunities. At the same time, you may notice which relationships drain you. Be mindful of your loyalty and invest it where it's valued. Today is about strengthening ties with people who uplift your spirit and share your vision. Surrounding yourself with positive influences helps your dreams gain momentum and strengthens your confidence.

Affirmation & Gratitude

I attract supportive friendships and collaborations, trusting community to uplift and inspire me.

Taurus
23-October-2026

Taurus, introspection takes priority today as the Sun enters Scorpio, your opposite sign. You may feel drawn to reflect on partnerships, trust, and the balance of give-and-take in your life. Hidden emotions may surface, asking to be acknowledged and released. This is a day for quiet, personal reflection rather than outward activity. Pay attention to dreams or intuitive nudges—they may hold guidance about your next steps. By honouring rest and stillness now, you prepare yourself for growth.

Affirmation & Gratitude

I honour rest and reflection, trusting stillness to bring clarity and renewal.

Taurus
24-October-2026

The Moon enters your sign, Taurus, filling you with renewed energy, vitality, and confidence. You may feel ready to set intentions, start a fresh project, or express your authenticity more fully. Others notice your calm strength and may be drawn to you because of it. This is a day for claiming your space unapologetically. Trust your instincts and lean into new beginnings. By embracing your worth and steady nature, you naturally attract the opportunities you deserve.

Affirmation & Gratitude

I shine with authenticity and confidence, trusting my steady energy to open new doors.

Taurus
25-October-2026

Taurus, today highlights resources and finances. You may feel motivated to review budgets, make practical plans, or organise possessions. But this energy also asks you to value yourself more deeply. Your patience, skills, and determination are your true wealth. Don't undervalue your worth or compare yourself to others—your journey is unfolding in its own perfect timing. A grounded decision made today may bring lasting benefits, especially in areas tied to long-term security.

Affirmation & Gratitude

I value my worth and trust my steady steps to build lasting prosperity.

Taurus
26-October-2026

Communication is spotlighted today, Taurus. Conversations may bring clarity, healing, or inspiration, provided you stay open to new perspectives. Writing, teaching, or sharing ideas is favoured now, as others respect your grounded voice. Listen carefully, as wisdom may come from unexpected sources. Short trips or errands may also spark new opportunities. Today is about balancing honesty with curiosity, ensuring that communication flows both ways. The universe reminds you that your words can inspire when used thoughtfully.

Affirmation & Gratitude

I communicate with clarity and openness, trusting dialogue to inspire growth and connection.

Taurus
27-October-2026

Taurus, home and family life take focus today. You may feel called to nurture your space, resolve domestic responsibilities, or strengthen emotional bonds with loved ones. A heartfelt conversation could bring healing if handled with patience. Even small actions like decluttering, cooking, or refreshing your environment restore peace and balance. Your home is not just a physical space—it's a reflection of your inner world. Creating harmony here strengthens you in every other aspect of life.

Affirmation & Gratitude

I create harmony in my home, trusting it as the foundation of my strength and peace.

Taurus
28-October-2026

Taurus, creativity and joy sparkle today. The cosmos encourages you to reconnect with your playful side through hobbies, art, or romance. If life has felt heavy lately, today brings a reminder that joy is medicine for your soul. Romantic connections deepen through lightheartedness and laughter, while personal projects may flow with extra inspiration. Allow yourself to step outside routine and indulge in activities that uplift your heart. Fun isn't a distraction—it's a vital source of balance and renewal.

Affirmation & Gratitude

I embrace joy and creativity, trusting play and love to nourish my spirit.

Taurus
29-October-2026

Health, routines, and organisation come into focus today. Taurus, you may feel motivated to refine your daily schedule, tend to responsibilities, or give your body the care it deserves. Don't pressure yourself with perfection—focus instead on small, sustainable changes that build resilience over time. Productivity flows best when paired with self-care. Whether through rest, nourishment, or movement, honour your body's needs. Today supports practical adjustments that strengthen both your well-being and your peace of mind.

Affirmation & Gratitude

I honour balance in my routines, trusting steady steps to build strength and clarity.

Taurus
30-October-2026

Relationships are spotlighted, Taurus. The cosmos asks you to examine balance and fairness within your partnerships. A heart-to-heart conversation may feel necessary to restore harmony or deepen trust. If single, you may notice new connections that resonate with your values. Authenticity is your key—don't hold back your truth for the sake of keeping peace. Vulnerability today opens the door to deeper bonds. This is about giving and receiving love in equal measure, creating relationships rooted in respect.

Affirmation & Gratitude

I welcome balanced and authentic relationships, trusting honesty to deepen my bonds.

Taurus
31-October-2026

Transformation energy surrounds you, Taurus. Matters of intimacy, shared resources, or hidden emotions may come to the forefront. You may be prompted to let go of old patterns, fears, or attachments that no longer serve your growth. While the process may feel intense, it carries the promise of renewal. Financial discussions could also be highlighted—approach them with clarity and integrity. Today is about courageously embracing change, knowing it paves the way for empowerment and fresh possibilities.

Affirmation & Gratitude

I release old patterns and embrace transformation, trusting renewal to strengthen me.

November 2026

Taurus
01-November-2026

Taurus, optimism and curiosity guide you today. You may feel called to explore new ideas, study, or plan adventures that broaden your perspective. Conversations with people from different backgrounds could spark inspiration. Your earthy nature values routine, but today invites you to expand beyond the familiar. Balance stability with exploration—you don't need to abandon your roots to grow. By saying yes to new opportunities, you enrich your journey and open your mind to fresh horizons.

Affirmation & Gratitude

I embrace curiosity and growth, trusting new experiences to enrich my journey.

Taurus
02-November-2026

Career and ambitions take centre stage today. Recognition for your reliability and persistence may come, or you may be asked to step into leadership. While responsibility could feel heavy, trust that your steady nature equips you to handle it with grace. This is a good day for strategic planning—reassess your goals and ensure they reflect your values. Avoid rushing; long-term success comes from consistency, not speed. Opportunities may arise if you step forward with quiet confidence.

Affirmation & Gratitude

I step steadily toward my goals, trusting persistence and patience to shape lasting success.

Taurus
03-November-2026

Friendships and social ties are highlighted today, Taurus. You may feel energised by connecting with like-minded people or collaborating on shared goals. Conversations within your community may inspire fresh insights, or group projects could gain momentum. At the same time, you may become aware of connections that no longer support your growth. Choose wisely where to invest your loyalty. By surrounding yourself with uplifting people, you create momentum for your dreams and strengthen your spirit.

Affirmation & Gratitude

I attract supportive friendships and collaborations, trusting community to inspire my growth.

Taurus
04-November-2026

Taurus, today invites reflection and solitude. You may feel less social, preferring to retreat into quiet spaces where you can recharge. This is a day to listen to your inner voice—your intuition has much to share now. Dreams, meditations, or even simple moments of stillness may reveal guidance. Old emotions could surface for release, allowing you to lighten your load. Don't view rest as inactivity—it's a form of preparation. By honouring silence today, you renew clarity and make room for fresh beginnings.

Affirmation & Gratitude

I honour stillness and reflection, trusting solitude to restore peace and clarity.

Taurus
05-November-2026

The Moon enters your sign, Taurus, energising you with confidence, vitality, and determination. You may feel ready to set intentions, launch a new project, or express yourself more authentically. Others are drawn to your calm strength, and opportunities may appear simply because of your presence. This is your chance to claim space without hesitation. Trust that your grounded nature is magnetic. Today is about stepping boldly into new beginnings and allowing your worth to shine through.

Affirmation & Gratitude

I shine with authenticity and confidence, trusting my steady energy to open new doors.

Taurus
06-November-2026

Taurus, resources and self-worth come into focus today. You may feel called to organise finances, review spending, or consider practical steps to strengthen long-term stability. This is also about recognising your inner wealth—your patience, skills, and persistence are invaluable. Avoid comparing yourself with others; your path is uniquely yours. A practical decision made now may have lasting benefits, especially if aligned with your values. Today is about trusting your worth and your ability to create abundance.

Affirmation & Gratitude

I value my worth and trust my steady actions to build lasting prosperity.

Taurus
07-November-2026

Communication is highlighted today, Taurus. Meaningful conversations could bring clarity or inspiration, and your words may carry more influence than usual. Writing, teaching, or sharing ideas flows easily, while listening carefully to others reveals insights you may have overlooked. Be flexible in your thinking—new perspectives may broaden your understanding. Short trips or chance encounters may spark opportunities. Today encourages you to balance your grounded wisdom with curiosity and openness, allowing you to grow through dialogue.

Affirmation & Gratitude

I communicate with clarity and openness, trusting dialogue to inspire growth and connection.

Taurus
08-November-2026

Home and family life take centre stage today. You may feel the urge to nurture your space, reconnect with loved ones, or resolve domestic matters. Emotional conversations may arise, but your patience can guide them toward healing. Even simple tasks like cooking, tidying, or rearranging your space bring a sense of comfort and balance. Your home is your sanctuary, and when it feels harmonious, you feel stronger in every other area of life. Today supports grounding through your roots.

Affirmation & Gratitude

I create harmony in my home, trusting it as the foundation of my peace and strength.

Taurus
09-November-2026

Taurus, joy and creativity are emphasised. The cosmos encourages you to indulge in hobbies, laughter, and romance. Your playful side is magnetic now, drawing in both people and inspiration. If responsibilities have felt heavy, today brings a reminder that fun is not frivolous—it's nourishment. Romantic bonds deepen through lighthearted connection, while creative outlets restore your energy. Give yourself permission to step away from duty for a while and revel in life's beauty.

Affirmation & Gratitude

I embrace joy and creativity, trusting play and love to nourish my spirit.

Taurus
10-November-2026

Health and routines take focus today, Taurus. You may feel motivated to organise, refine, or create more balance in your schedule. Your body may also signal its needs—whether that's more rest, better nourishment, or physical activity. Don't try to change everything at once; instead, focus on steady improvements you can maintain. Work tasks benefit from your methodical nature, but remember to balance effort with rest. Today supports creating routines that sustain you for the long term.

Affirmation & Gratitude

I honour balance in my routines, trusting steady habits to strengthen my well-being.

Taurus
11-November-2026

Taurus, relationships are in focus today. You may feel called to reflect on fairness and balance within your partnerships. A heartfelt conversation may bring clarity, helping you or a loved one better understand each other's needs. Vulnerability deepens trust, so don't be afraid to express your truth. If single, new opportunities for connection may surface—be open to genuine encounters. Authenticity is key. Today's energy supports creating bonds based on honesty, patience, and mutual respect.

Affirmation & Gratitude

I welcome balanced and authentic relationships, trusting openness to deepen my connections.

Taurus
12-November-2026

Transformation energy rises, Taurus. Matters tied to intimacy, shared resources, or old fears may come to the forefront. Though intensity may feel uncomfortable, it offers a path toward renewal. Financial commitments or deep emotions may require your attention, and honesty will serve you best. Letting go of outdated patterns is not easy, but it makes way for strength and empowerment. Trust that what you release today creates space for fresh opportunities. Change is not the end—it's the beginning of something better.

Affirmation & Gratitude

I release what no longer serves me, trusting transformation to bring clarity and empowerment.

Taurus
13-November-2026

Taurus, expansion and curiosity guide you. You may feel inspired to explore new ideas, connect with different cultures, or dive into learning. Travel planning or study is favoured, but even small changes in routine can broaden your perspective. Conversations may spark excitement and remind you of life's bigger picture. Your earthy nature prefers security, but today the stars ask you to blend stability with exploration. Growth happens when you step outside your comfort zone with courage.

Affirmation & Gratitude

I embrace curiosity and growth, trusting new experiences to expand my wisdom.

Taurus
14-November-2026

Career and long-term ambitions take the spotlight. Taurus, your persistence may be recognised, or a leadership opportunity could be presented to you. While responsibility might feel heavy, your steady nature ensures you can handle it. This is also a powerful day for reassessing goals—are they aligned with what you truly value? Avoid chasing quick wins; your strength lies in consistent effort. Trust that each step you take is building a foundation for lasting success.

Affirmation & Gratitude

I step steadily toward my ambitions, trusting persistence and patience to shape my future.

Taurus
15-November-2026

Friendships and social connections are highlighted. Taurus, you may feel energised by collaboration or group activities that inspire your spirit. Conversations with supportive friends could spark new ideas, or you may feel motivated to contribute to a community project. At the same time, you might sense which relationships no longer serve your growth. Invest your energy where it is valued. By surrounding yourself with uplifting people, you strengthen your own confidence and vision.

Affirmation & Gratitude

I attract supportive friendships and collaborations, trusting community to inspire joy and growth.

Taurus
16-November-2026

Introspection is favoured today, Taurus. You may crave solitude, preferring quiet over activity. This is a powerful day for reflection, meditation, or journaling. Dreams or subtle signs may deliver guidance, so trust your inner voice. Emotions may rise, offering release and renewal. Stillness is not a waste—it strengthens clarity and prepares you for new beginnings. Honour your need for rest and know that slowing down today is a step toward greater peace.

Affirmation & Gratitude

I honour stillness and reflection, trusting solitude to restore my clarity and peace.

Taurus
17-November-2026

The Moon enters your sign, Taurus, bringing fresh energy, confidence, and a sense of renewal. You may feel inspired to take bold steps, set personal intentions, or embrace a new project. Others notice your calm presence, and opportunities may arise because of your authenticity. This is your moment to embody your worth and step forward unapologetically. Trust your steady nature—your grounded energy is magnetic and opens doors when you stand firmly in who you are.

Affirmation & Gratitude

I shine with confidence and authenticity, trusting my steady nature to guide new beginnings.

Taurus
18-November-2026

Taurus, today highlights your resources and sense of self-worth. You may feel motivated to review budgets, strengthen financial plans, or take steps toward security. But this is also about inner wealth—your patience, talents, and resilience. Don't diminish your value by comparing yourself to others. Small, practical actions made now can bring lasting results, especially if they align with your long-term goals. Trust your steady approach—it creates abundance step by step. The universe reminds you that valuing yourself is the first step toward prosperity.

Affirmation & Gratitude

I value my worth and trust my steady steps to create lasting prosperity.

Taurus
19-November-2026

Communication is spotlighted today. Taurus, conversations may bring clarity, healing, or fresh inspiration. Writing, teaching, or sharing your thoughts flows naturally, and others respect your calm, grounded perspective. Stay open to listening—wisdom can arrive from unexpected places. Short trips or errands may also spark insights or opportunities. Your voice has influence, so use it with honesty and care. Today encourages you to balance expressing yourself with staying curious, creating space for growth through dialogue.

Affirmation & Gratitude

I communicate with clarity and openness, trusting dialogue to inspire growth and connection.

Taurus
20-November-2026

Taurus, your home and family life take focus. You may feel called to nurture your environment, resolve domestic matters, or connect more deeply with loved ones. Emotional conversations may arise, but your patience and steady nature can bring healing and harmony. Even small acts like cooking, tidying, or refreshing your space restore balance. Your home is your sanctuary—it reflects your inner world. By bringing peace to your private life, you strengthen every other part of your journey.

Affirmation & Gratitude

I create peace and harmony in my home, trusting it as the foundation of my strength.

Taurus
21-November-2026

Creativity and joy are highlighted today, Taurus. The stars invite you to indulge in hobbies, playfulness, and romance. If life has felt heavy, this is your reminder that joy is healing. Romantic connections may blossom, or existing bonds may feel lighter through laughter and affection. Creative pursuits also feel fulfilling now, offering both inspiration and balance. Allow yourself to shine through play and self-expression—these moments remind you that happiness is a vital part of growth.

Affirmation & Gratitude

I embrace joy and creativity, trusting play and love to nourish my spirit.

Taurus
22-November-2026

Taurus, routines, health, and organisation are emphasised today. You may feel motivated to refine habits, improve balance, or care for your body more attentively. This isn't about doing everything at once—your strength lies in steady improvements. Productivity is favoured, but don't neglect rest. By blending effort with care, you create resilience that lasts. The Sun also moves into Sagittarius today, highlighting transformation, shared resources, and deeper trust over the coming month. Expect shifts that lead to renewal.

Affirmation & Gratitude

I honour balance in my routines, trusting steady habits to build long-term strength.

Taurus
23-November-2026

Relationships are in focus today. Taurus, you may feel drawn to reflect on fairness, openness, and authenticity within your partnerships. Someone close may need your support, but ensure your needs are also respected. Honest conversations bring clarity now. If single, new connections may appear that align with your values. Harmony doesn't mean avoiding conflict—it comes from showing up truthfully. Today's energy encourages balance, where love and respect flow in both directions.

Affirmation & Gratitude

I welcome authentic and balanced relationships, trusting openness to deepen my bonds.

Taurus
24-November-2026

Transformation energy rises today, Taurus. You may feel prompted to release old fears, review shared resources, or face deeper emotions that have lingered. While this can feel intense, it holds the promise of empowerment. Financial or emotional entanglements may require honesty and courage. Transformation clears away what no longer serves you, making space for growth and clarity. By leaning into change, you reclaim your strength. Today is about embracing renewal, even if it feels unfamiliar.

Affirmation & Gratitude

I release what no longer serves, trusting transformation to bring renewal and empowerment.

Taurus
25-November-2026

Taurus, optimism flows today as the stars encourage you to expand your horizons. You may feel drawn to study, explore, or connect with people who broaden your perspective. Travel plans may surface, or you might feel inspired by a conversation that shifts your outlook. Your earthy nature prefers the familiar, but today reminds you that growth requires curiosity. By blending security with exploration, you enrich your journey. A fresh perspective can help you see current challenges in a new light.

Affirmation & Gratitude

I embrace curiosity and growth, trusting new horizons to enrich my journey.

Taurus
26-November-2026

Career and ambitions come into focus today. Taurus, recognition for your steady persistence may arrive, or new responsibilities may call for your leadership. While pressure might feel heavy, your grounded approach ensures you can handle it. Use this energy to review your long-term goals—are they aligned with your values and vision? Avoid chasing fast results. Instead, focus on building a legacy step by step. Your calm steadiness inspires others, and opportunities may arise because of your reliability.

Affirmation & Gratitude

I step confidently toward my goals, trusting persistence and patience to shape lasting success.

Taurus
27-November-2026

Friendships and community connections are highlighted, Taurus. You may feel uplifted by supportive people who share your values or inspired to collaborate on group projects. Conversations within your social circles may spark fresh ideas or opportunities. At the same time, you may notice which connections no longer energise you. Be discerning—invest your loyalty in relationships that value and encourage you. Today is about surrounding yourself with people who help your dreams take root and grow stronger.

Affirmation & Gratitude

I attract supportive friendships and collaborations, trusting community to inspire my growth.

Taurus
28-November-2026

Taurus, introspection is favoured today. You may feel quieter, preferring solitude and reflection over busy activity. This is an excellent time for journaling, meditation, or connecting with your inner wisdom. Dreams or intuitive signs may carry important messages, so pay attention to subtle guidance. Old emotions may resurface for release—acknowledge them, then let them go. Don't confuse rest with stagnation; stillness is what strengthens your clarity. Today is about recharging your spirit for the new beginnings ahead.

Affirmation & Gratitude

I honour stillness and reflection, trusting solitude to restore my clarity and peace.

Taurus
29-November-2026

The Moon enters your sign, Taurus, filling you with renewed confidence, vitality, and authenticity. You may feel ready to embrace fresh projects, take bold steps, or show up more fully as yourself. Others notice your calm steadiness and may be drawn to your energy. This is a day to set intentions that reflect your true desires. Trust that your grounded presence is magnetic—by honouring your worth, you naturally attract the opportunities you deserve.

Affirmation & Gratitude

I shine with confidence and authenticity, trusting my steady nature to guide new beginnings.

Taurus
30-November-2026

Taurus, resources and self-worth are in focus. You may feel prompted to review budgets, set long-term plans, or organise your material life. But the deeper theme is recognising the value you carry within—your patience, skills, and persistence are powerful assets. Avoid comparison with others; your progress unfolds at the right pace. A small, practical choice made today could bring lasting benefits. The stars remind you that abundance is both material and spiritual—honour both sides equally.

Affirmation & Gratitude

I value my worth and trust my steady actions to create lasting prosperity.

December 2026

Taurus
01-December-2026

Communication is spotlighted today. Taurus, important conversations may arise that bring clarity, resolve misunderstandings, or open new opportunities. Writing, teaching, or sharing ideas flows easily now, as your grounded wisdom resonates with others. Be mindful of your tone and stay open to listening—insights may come from unexpected places. Short trips or casual encounters could also prove meaningful. Today is about balancing curiosity with practical wisdom, creating space for connection and growth through dialogue.

Affirmation & Gratitude

I communicate with clarity and openness, trusting dialogue to inspire growth and understanding.

Taurus
02-December-2026

Taurus, your home and family life take focus today. You may feel pulled to nurture your environment, handle domestic responsibilities, or reconnect with loved ones. Conversations could reveal underlying emotions, but your patience can guide them toward resolution. Even small acts—like cooking, tidying, or adding beauty to your space—restore comfort and grounding. Your home reflects your inner peace, and creating harmony here strengthens every other part of your journey. Today is about strengthening your roots and cultivating stability.

Affirmation & Gratitude

I create peace and harmony in my home, trusting it as the foundation of my strength.

Taurus
03-December-2026

Joy, creativity, and romance are highlighted, Taurus. The cosmos encourages you to set aside seriousness and embrace activities that uplift your spirit. Whether through art, hobbies, or simple laughter, you are reminded that joy is essential, not optional. Romantic energy flows easily, deepening bonds through playfulness and affection. Self-expression is healing now, so allow yourself to shine without hesitation. By tapping into beauty and fun, you recharge your energy and attract positivity into your life.

Affirmation & Gratitude

I embrace joy and creativity, trusting play and love to renew my spirit.

Taurus
04-December-2026

Taurus, health, routines, and organisation are spotlighted. You may feel motivated to refine habits, reorganise your schedule, or focus on well-being. Avoid overwhelming yourself—progress comes from steady, sustainable actions. Your body may signal its needs now, whether rest, nourishment, or exercise. Work matters also benefit from your persistence and methodical nature. By blending self-care with productivity, you build resilience that supports long-term stability. The stars encourage you to honour both effort and rest equally.

Affirmation & Gratitude

I honour balance in my routines, trusting steady habits to build long-term strength.

Taurus
05-December-2026

Relationships come into focus today, Taurus. The stars encourage you to reflect on honesty, fairness, and openness in your partnerships. A heartfelt discussion may bring deeper understanding or reveal where balance is needed. If single, you may notice opportunities for meaningful connections that align with your values. Don't shy away from vulnerability—it deepens trust. Today's energy supports investing in authentic relationships that uplift and support you while also honouring your needs.

Affirmation & Gratitude

I welcome authentic and balanced relationships, trusting honesty to deepen my bonds.

Taurus
06-December-2026

Transformation energy surrounds you. Taurus, matters of intimacy, trust, or shared resources may arise, prompting you to look at what needs release. This is a day to face fears or outdated patterns with courage. Though intensity may feel uncomfortable, it clears the way for growth. Financial matters may also need review —approach them with honesty. Transformation isn't about loss; it's about renewal. By leaning into vulnerability, you reclaim your power and strengthen your future path.

Affirmation & Gratitude

I release what no longer serves, trusting transformation to bring renewal and empowerment.

Taurus
07-December-2026

Taurus, optimism and expansion light up your day. You may feel drawn to explore, learn, or plan something new that broadens your world. Conversations with people from different walks of life could spark exciting insights. Travel planning or study is favoured, but even small shifts in perspective can refresh your spirit. Your steady nature provides the grounding to explore without losing stability. Say yes to opportunities that open your heart and mind—you're ready for new experiences.

Affirmation & Gratitude

I embrace curiosity and growth, trusting new horizons to enrich my life.

Taurus
08-December-2026

Career and long-term goals are spotlighted today, Taurus. Recognition for your persistence may come, or you may feel called to take on a leadership role. While the responsibility could feel heavy, your calm determination is your strength. This is a great day to review your goals and align them with your values. Avoid rushing—success for you is built brick by brick. Trust that your efforts are shaping a legacy that will last. Others admire your reliability and integrity.

Affirmation & Gratitude

I step confidently toward my ambitions, trusting persistence and patience to shape lasting success.

Taurus
09-December-2026

Taurus, friendships and community ties are highlighted today. You may feel uplifted by connecting with people who share your values or inspired to collaborate on shared goals. Conversations within your circle may spark fresh insights or help you see possibilities in a new light. At the same time, you might notice which relationships no longer align with your energy. Invest your loyalty where it is truly valued. By surrounding yourself with supportive people, you create momentum and joy on your path.

Affirmation & Gratitude

I attract supportive friendships and collaborations, trusting community to inspire my growth.

Taurus
10-December-2026

Taurus, today invites rest and reflection. You may crave quiet moments away from the noise of daily life. Intuitive nudges, dreams, or synchronicities could carry valuable messages, so pay attention to subtle signs. Old emotions may rise, asking to be acknowledged and released. Don't see this stillness as wasted time—pausing restores clarity and prepares you for fresh beginnings. Honour your need for solitude; it allows you to return to your path feeling lighter, clearer, and more grounded.

Affirmation & Gratitude

I honour stillness and solitude, trusting reflection to restore my peace and clarity.

Taurus
11-December-2026

The Moon moves into your sign today, Taurus, energising you with confidence, vitality, and fresh perspective. You may feel ready to take bold steps, start something new, or show up more fully as your authentic self. Others notice your steady presence, and opportunities may be drawn to you simply because of your calm magnetism. This is your moment to claim space and set intentions that align with your values. Don't downplay your worth—shine boldly today.

Affirmation & Gratitude

I shine with confidence and authenticity, trusting my steady nature to guide new beginnings.

Taurus
12-December-2026

Taurus, resources and self-worth are in the spotlight. You may feel motivated to review your finances, make practical decisions, or explore new ways to build stability. But this energy also reminds you of your inner wealth—your persistence, patience, and talents are priceless. Avoid comparing your journey with others; your progress unfolds at the right pace. Small, steady steps made today will lead to long-term abundance. Trust your ability to create prosperity while honouring your values.

Affirmation & Gratitude

I value my worth and trust my steady steps to build lasting prosperity.

Taurus
13-December-2026

Communication is favoured today, Taurus. Conversations may bring clarity or healing, provided you remain open-minded and patient. Writing, teaching, or sharing your thoughts could flow easily, and others respect your grounded wisdom. Short trips or unexpected encounters may spark opportunities, so stay flexible. Your words carry weight now, but listening is just as important. Balance your desire to share with your ability to learn, and you'll uncover valuable insights that support your growth.

Affirmation & Gratitude

I communicate with clarity and openness, trusting dialogue to inspire connection and growth.

Taurus
14-December-2026

Home and family matters take focus. Taurus, you may feel the need to nurture your space, reconnect with loved ones, or resolve domestic issues. Emotional conversations could arise, but your calm presence can guide them toward healing. Even simple acts—like cooking, tidying, or refreshing your home—restore balance and comfort. Your home is your foundation, and when it feels peaceful, every other part of life feels steadier. Today supports strengthening both your sanctuary and your closest bonds.

Affirmation & Gratitude

I create harmony in my home, trusting it as the foundation of my strength.

Taurus
15-December-2026

Taurus, joy and creativity are highlighted. The cosmos encourages you to embrace play, hobbies, or romance as nourishment for your spirit. Life is not only about responsibilities—it's also about delighting in beauty and love. Romantic connections may flourish, or creative projects may feel especially fulfilling. Don't underestimate the healing power of laughter and self-expression. By embracing your playful side, you recharge and inspire others with your warmth. Today is about honouring the joy that lives within you.

Affirmation & Gratitude

I embrace joy and creativity, trusting play and love to uplift and restore my spirit.

Taurus
16-December-2026

Taurus, health and routines take priority today. You may feel motivated to refine your schedule, bring order to your tasks, or adopt new habits that improve your well-being. Don't overburden yourself with unrealistic goals—focus instead on small, steady steps that create lasting balance. Your body may also signal its needs, whether through rest, nourishment, or gentle activity. Productivity flows more easily when it's balanced with self-care. Today encourages you to invest in practices that support both resilience and peace.

Affirmation & Gratitude

I honour balance in my routines, trusting steady habits to strengthen my body, mind, and spirit.

Taurus
17-December-2026

Relationships are highlighted today, Taurus. The stars ask you to reflect on how balance and fairness play out in your partnerships. Someone close may need your support, but be mindful to honour your own needs too. A conversation could bring deeper understanding if approached with patience. If single, new connections may feel promising, especially if they align with your values. Authenticity is the key to lasting bonds. Today favours honesty, vulnerability, and trust in your interactions.

Affirmation & Gratitude

I welcome authentic and balanced relationships, trusting openness to deepen my bonds.

Taurus
18-December-2026

Taurus, today carries transformational energy. Matters involving intimacy, trust, or shared resources may rise to the surface. This could feel intense, but it's also an opportunity for growth. Financial commitments may need review, or emotions you've kept hidden could demand release. Transformation isn't about loss—it's about clearing space for renewal and empowerment. The stars encourage you to let go of what no longer serves you so you can reclaim your strength and move forward with clarity.

Affirmation & Gratitude

I release what no longer serves, trusting transformation to bring empowerment and clarity.

Taurus
19-December-2026

Optimism and exploration guide you today. Taurus, you may feel inspired to broaden your horizons through study, travel, or conversations that expand your perspective. Growth often comes when you step outside your comfort zone, and today supports that. Your grounded energy ensures you won't lose stability while exploring new possibilities. Be open to fresh ideas and experiences—they could spark long-term inspiration. Today is about balancing security with curiosity and trusting that both can coexist harmoniously.

Affirmation & Gratitude

I embrace curiosity and growth, trusting new experiences to enrich my path.

Taurus
20-December-2026

Taurus, career and ambitions are spotlighted. Recognition for your persistence may come, or a new responsibility may place you in a leadership position. While pressure may feel heavy, remember that persistence is your greatest strength. Today is excellent for long term planning—review your professional path and ensure it aligns with your values. Avoid rushing; lasting success is built step by step. Your reliability is admired by others, and new doors may open because of it.

Affirmation & Gratitude

I move steadily toward my goals, trusting patience and persistence to shape my legacy.

Taurus
21-December-2026

Friendships and community ties are in focus today. You may feel energised by connecting with like-minded people, joining group projects, or collaborating with those who share your vision. Conversations may spark fresh insights, helping you see opportunities you hadn't considered. At the same time, you may recognise which connections no longer support your growth. Invest your loyalty where it's reciprocated. By surrounding yourself with uplifting people, you strengthen your dreams and add momentum to your journey.

Affirmation & Gratitude

I attract supportive friendships and collaborations, trusting community to inspire my growth.

Taurus
22-December-2026

Taurus, introspection is favoured as the Sun enters Capricorn, shifting focus to expansion, wisdom, and long-term vision. You may feel quieter, preferring to reflect on recent lessons and plan for what lies ahead. This is a powerful day for journaling, meditation, or simply giving yourself time to think. Don't dismiss stillness—it creates clarity for the new chapter approaching. Dreams or intuitive nudges may offer guidance now. Honour this pause as a sacred part of your growth cycle.

Affirmation & Gratitude

I honour stillness and reflection, trusting quiet moments to guide my next steps.

Taurus
23-December-2026

Taurus, the Moon enters your sign today, infusing you with vitality, confidence, and fresh determination. You may feel ready to set intentions, begin new projects, or express yourself more authentically. Others notice your steady, grounded energy, and this draws opportunities toward you. Don't hold back from stepping into visibility—you have something meaningful to share. This is an excellent day to affirm your worth and take practical steps that align with your bigger vision. Trust your instincts; they won't lead you astray.

Affirmation & Gratitude

I shine with confidence and authenticity, trusting my steady nature to guide new beginnings.

Taurus
24-December-2026

Taurus, resources and self-worth are spotlighted. You may feel motivated to review finances, organise possessions, or create greater stability through practical choices. But the deeper theme is recognising your own value. Don't undervalue your skills, patience, and persistence—these are the true foundations of abundance. Avoid comparing yourself to others; your path is uniquely yours. A grounded choice made today may set the stage for long-term prosperity. Honour your worth, and abundance naturally follows.

Affirmation & Gratitude

I value my worth and trust my steady steps to create lasting prosperity.

Taurus
25-December-2026

Communication is emphasised today. Taurus, heartfelt conversations may bring connection, healing, or joy. This is a day for sharing thoughts and listening deeply to others. Writing, storytelling, or teaching may also feel natural now. Stay open to unexpected encounters—they may carry important insights or blessings. Your words have weight, and when paired with your calm patience, they can soothe and inspire. Let dialogue be a bridge that strengthens understanding and spreads warmth on this special day.

Affirmation & Gratitude

I communicate with clarity and kindness, trusting dialogue to create deeper connection.

Taurus
26-December-2026

Home and family take focus today, Taurus. You may feel drawn to nurture your living space or connect with loved ones in meaningful ways. Emotional conversations could bring healing, while practical efforts—like tidying, cooking, or refreshing your surroundings restore peace. Your home is not just where you live; it's your sanctuary. By tending to it, you reinforce stability in all areas of life. Today supports strengthening bonds and creating an environment that mirrors your inner calm.

Affirmation & Gratitude

I create harmony in my home, trusting it as the foundation of my peace and strength.

Taurus
27-December-2026

Joy, creativity, and romance sparkle today. Taurus, you're encouraged to set aside responsibilities and lean into playfulness. Creative pursuits, art, or music may bring inspiration, while lighthearted moments with loved ones deepen bonds. Romance feels especially sweet now, strengthened by laughter and affection. Fun is not frivolous—it is medicine for the soul. Today reminds you to prioritise what uplifts your spirit and fills your life with beauty and joy.

Affirmation & Gratitude

I embrace joy and creativity, trusting play and love to nourish my spirit.

Taurus
28-December-2026

Taurus, health, routines, and organisation are in focus. You may feel inspired to refine habits, balance responsibilities, or care for your body more attentively. Productivity flows when paired with self-care, so avoid overloading yourself. Instead, aim for simple, steady improvements. Your grounded persistence makes long-term success possible. This is a perfect day to align your daily rhythm with your deeper goals, ensuring that both your body and spirit feel supported.

Affirmation & Gratitude

I honour balance in my routines, trusting steady habits to strengthen my resilience.

Taurus
29-December-2026

Relationships are highlighted today, Taurus. The stars encourage you to reflect on how you show up in partnerships and whether balance is being maintained. Someone close may seek your attention, or you may feel the need to clarify your own needs. Vulnerability and honesty can lead to greater trust. If single, you may notice opportunities for new, meaningful connections. Harmony comes when both sides feel respected. Today's energy supports building relationships that are authentic and uplifting.

Affirmation & Gratitude

I welcome balanced and authentic relationships, trusting openness to deepen my connections.

Taurus
30-December-2026

Transformation energy is strong today, Taurus. You may feel called to release lingering fears, insecurities, or attachments that have quietly held you back this year. Matters of intimacy, trust, or shared resources may surface, asking for your honest attention. While this can feel intense, it's also deeply empowering. Think of today as a final clearing before you step into the fresh energy of the new year. By letting go, you create space for renewal. Transformation is not about loss—it's about stepping into a truer, stronger version of yourself.

Affirmation & Gratitude

I release what no longer serves, trusting transformation to open space for renewal and strength.

Taurus
31-December-2026

Taurus, the year ends on an expansive note. The stars encourage you to reflect on the growth you've achieved and the lessons you've embraced. You may feel drawn to dream big about the year ahead, setting intentions that inspire hope and balance. Conversations with others may bring encouragement, or you may find wisdom in looking back with gratitude. This is a day for optimism, faith, and trust in the journey ahead. You are closing one chapter with grace and preparing to begin another with courage.

Affirmation & Gratitude

I welcome the new year with hope, trusting growth and steady steps to guide my path forward.

www.ingramcontent.com/pod-product-compliance
Lightning Source LLC
Chambersburg PA
CBHW071146070526
44584CB00019B/2674